The Power
of Judgment

Critical Skills for Wiser Living

RYAN A. KUETER

CONTENTS

PREFACE 1

PART I:
ASSESSING JUDGMENT 10
Good Judgment 13

1 **COGNITIVE LIMITATIONS** 16
Mental Models 17
Cognitive Limitations 19
Executive Ability 20
Memory 23
Emotions 25
Intuition 26
Mental Logic 29
Logical Errors 30
Critical Skills 33

2 **RESEARCH METHODS** 36
Choices 37
Quality of Information 39
Subjective Experience vs. Objective Reality 40
Gossip 42
Studies & Research 45
Suspending Judgment 48
Error Checking 49
Modeling Techniques 51
Scenario Analysis 52
Cost-Benefit Analysis 54
Data Modeling & Artificial Intelligence 57
Reality Testing 60
Critical Skills 61

PART II:
ASSESSING RESPONSIBILITY   64

3   **PERSONAL RESPONSIBILITY**   65
Defining Responsibility   66
Learning Responsibility   67
Attributing Responsibility   68
Product of Circumstance   70
Product of Choice   71
Answering for Decisions   72
Character Defenses   73
Blaming   75
Rationalization   77
Deception   78
Obstruction   80
Taking Responsibility   81
Giving Responsibility   83
Critical Skills   84

4   **SOCIAL RESPONSIBILITY**   86
Forms of Social Responsibility   87
Responsible Use of Power   88
Systems of Accountability   92
Responsible Policy   94
Responsible Use of Technology   99
Critical Skills   100

PART III:
ASSESSING CAPABILITIES   103

5   **THE HUMAN CONDITION**   105
The Science of Behavior   106
Consequential Abilities   109

Mindsets & the Effects of Discouragement   110
Developmental Solutions   114
Critical Skills   116

6   **SKILLS DEVELOPMENT**   118
The Principle of Gradual Improvement   119
Habits   121
Skills   125
Role Skills   127
Character Development   129
The Learning Curve   131
Confidence Assessment   132
Measuring Ability   135
Skills Tests   138
Critical Skills   141

PART IV:
ASSESSING MOTIVES   144

7   **A THEORY OF MOTIVATION**   145
Theories of Motivation   146
The Private Interest Theory of Motivation   149
Value Creation   152
The Effect of Gains & Losses   155
Emotional Consequences   158
Inequity   161
Critical Skills   164

8   **MOTIVATING PRODUCTIVITY**   167
Productivity   168
Cognitive Focus   168
Goal Setting   170
Time Management   171

	Creativity	174
	Motivating Others	176
	Incentive-Based Motivation	178
	Encouragement & Discouragement	181
	Commitment	184
	Critical Skills	185
9	**MOTIVATING COOPERATION**	189
	Healthy Relationships	190
	Communication Skills	191
	Emotional Skills	192
	Trust	194
	Conflict Resolution Skills	196
	Critical Skills	198
	PART V:	
	ASSESSING STRESS & ADVERSITY	200
10	**STRESS MANAGEMENT**	204
	Stress Management	205
	Fear & Distress	207
	Stressors	209
	Chronic Stress	210
	Stress Management Techniques	212
	Accepting Loss	214
	Positive Thinking	215
	Attitude	216
	Recreation	217
	Critical Skills	219
11	**MENTAL HEALTH**	221
	Mental Effects of Adversity	222
	Childhood Adversity	224

CONTENTS

Harmful Biases   230
Employment Adversity   234
Social Isolation Adversity   238
Mental Disorders   240
Critical Skills   245

REFERENCES   248
INDEX   257

PREFACE

Thank you for reading the *Power of Judgment: Critical Skills for Wiser Living*. The word homo sapiens, which is often used as the biological classification for modern humans, means wise man. But how wise are people, really? If wisdom is the ability to use good judgment, then how good are people at recognizing poor judgment when they see it, in their own decisions or in those of other people? And, more importantly, do people know how to use better judgment when they need to? These are important questions for both powerful people who make impactful world-changing decisions, and for average people who are trying to create better lives for themselves. In this book, we explore the science of judgment to understand how to spot bad judgment and techniques for using better judgment when making risky or impactful decisions.

Human judgment is central to understanding and changing behavior for a number of reasons. It influences how you view your options, make decisions, predict consequences, and succeed or fail in your endeavors. No other subject is more central to human development, and the problems people face, than judgment. It's one of the most powerful social forces shaping people's lives in ways they may not understand. How you are judged often determines your fate, whether you are hired, promoted, or fired, the amount of money you make, who you marry, what career you pursue, and whether you could make a strong leader. People fear being judged. They fear admitting to mistakes, talking about their preferences, or talking about mental conditions or diseases, because of how they may be judged by other people.

Human judgment can also be the root of all evil. Social problems, as they are defined in this book, are problems that have a negative impact on human populations, like crime, corruption, racial and ethnic injustices, mass shootings, pollution, and inhuman treatment. And today, television is rife with stories about racial injustice, reducing the stigma of mental illness, and cyberbullying, all of which are directly caused by judgment. Arguably, if scientists had one challenge that could improve our world, and leave a lasting impression on the future of humanity, it would be to figure out how to improve judgment and decision-making.

An obvious example of how bad judgment causes bad behavior is crime. You likely have better ways of obtaining what you want without committing crimes that could land you in prison. Crimes leave behind victims who are, then, motivated to get justice, or to prevent the perpetrator from doing it again. But poor judgment does not just apply to criminals, or people who are uneducated. Powerful people in leadership positions, who may be well-educated and entrusted to make critical decisions, also use bad judgment.

People who are entrusted to make important decisions often have extensive education, training, and experience that enables them to exercise better judgment and make calculated decisions. But sometimes, especially with topics they know very little about, they can make serious mistakes that do harm, or they use their power to hurt or take advantage of people. And it's disappointing to watch powerful people, who are sometimes highly educated, make terrible decisions simply because they don't want to admit their ignorance, research a subject, or consult with an expert, to make a better decision. In those instances, those decision-makers would certainly benefit by knowing how to use better judgment.

You may not even realize it, but many of the daily problems that drive you a little crazy are actually caused by human judgment. Consider an example in which a man, let's call him Bob, is an Engineer who seems to do everything right in his career and personal life. He is highly intelligent, responsible, and goes out of his way to help people. But one day, he confronts his manager and points out that guidelines are not being followed and customer's lives may be in danger. His manager seemed annoyed by Bob's criticism and simply ignored his concern. So, Bob files a complaint to Human Resources (HR).

When looking at the report, the HR person, let's call her Sandra, believes that Bob is lying. When reading Bob's report, she doubted that would ever happen because Bob's manager is smarter than that and the management at the company knew what they were doing. So, rather than looking into the matter, Sandra has already formed her own conclusions and recommended that Bob be terminated from his position. Later, after an investigation, management discovered that Bob was telling the truth. And when the business owner visits Sandra, she said that she didn't think it was fair to her because she didn't know that. Of course, she is still responsible for failing to look into Bob's report.

This example of poor judgment is not only harmful, it's easily preventable. Someone, like Sandra, may even be inclined to believe that things, like this, don't happen, or that

Bob would have grounds for a lawsuit. But this actually follows a very typical pattern of behavior that's not uncommon in real-world circumstances. And depending on the situation, the consequences could be far worse. In this instance, Bob is not only the victim of poor judgment, he may continue to be the victim of poor judgment as he looks for work elsewhere. When Bob tries to explain his experience to hiring managers and recruiters, they immediately suspect he must have done something more to deserve being fired.

The problem is, many hiring managers and recruiters may be biased in that they may automatically assume the employer is operating responsibly, so all blame and suspicion is put on Bob. And hiring managers may begin to wonder what Bob is really doing to cause these problems. But the real source of Bob's problems, in this case, is not his own behavior, but instead the way he is judged and treated, first, by his employer and, secondly, by hiring managers and recruiters. And when they fail to consider this possibility, and continue misattributing the problem to Bob's behavior, it only makes the problem worse.

When people know very little about something, they tend to make decisions based on the small amount of information they have, whether that is a superficial detail or a work history on a resume. But the truth about people's lives goes much deeper. If hiring managers are unable to look beyond the superficial details and get to the underlying facts regarding Bob's own record and performance, then they will miss how reliable and strong of an employee he really is. No matter how good of an expert Bob is, his career path is irreversibly changed. And if hiring managers continue treating Bob the same, that change may be for the worse.

All of these problems are directly attributed to bad judgment on the part of the managers. Bad judgment, in these instances, occurs because people want to believe something is true based on their own life experiences, but don't actually look into the facts of the matter. Ironically, that weak judgment almost always tends to benefit the worst, and most unscrupulous, people. In Bob's case, it benefited his former manager. But con-artists also exploit weaknesses in judgment to unwittingly take advantage of unsuspecting victims. Abusers, and perpetrators of child abuse or sexual assault, are sometimes automatically believed over their victims, especially when the perpetrator is someone who appears to be reputable and is striving for social approval. In those instances, rather than bringing about justice, weak judgment actually protects the perpetrators and creates more injustice.

One of my main reasons for writing this book is the fact that people are able to use better judgment, but often never learn how or why. Bad judgment is a serious problem that leads to a variety of social problems and needs to be addressed. After entering the workforce more than twenty years ago, I began exploring ways to improve my own decision-making. Some of my early exercises, adopted from my own observations, included 1) recognizing what I don't know, and 2) getting the facts necessary to know what I'm talking about. Using better judgment requires more than these two exercises, as we will see in later chapters. But to this day, these simple exercises have helped me tremendously by decreasing my error-rate, improving the quality of my work, helping me to be more responsible, understanding people's motives, and motivating me to study more rigorously. During these last twenty years, my experience has shown me that it is absolutely possible to improve judgment and decision-making, but only when people know how.

i

In This Book

Each part of this book covers a skill that helps you to exercise better judgment, and make knowledgeable decisions with more predictable consequences, in circumstances where you have little information and a lot of uncertainty. Many of these skills are considered the human factors of success and failure because deficits in any one of these skills usually causes projects to fail, relationships to crumble, social problems, and unnecessary distress that is toxic to your mental health. Each chapter ends with a section on critical skills that offers suggestions on how to practice exercising better judgment based on the material covered in the chapter.

Part I: Assessing Judgment looks at how to improve the accuracy and truthfulness of your judgment. This not only applies to being critical of other people but, more importantly, being critical of yourself and your own judgment when it matters. In *Chapter 1: Cognitive Limitations,* we look at how poor judgment is often caused by the human brain's limited capacity to construct an accurate representation of the world and how it works. More specifically, poor judgment is caused by missing information that leads to false beliefs, wrong assumptions, bad ideas, and poor decisions. In *Chapter 2: Research Techniques,* we look at how to overcome many of these cognitive limitations by applying some research techniques that can enable you to reduce risk and improve certainty in your decisions.

Part II: Assessing Responsibility looks at the ability to correctly assign blame to oneself, to other people, or to external causes. In *Chapter 3: Personal Responsibility* we look some reasons people sometimes struggle with the ability to correctly assign blame. *Chapter 4: Social Responsibility* explores the impact that decisions have on one's life, the lives other people, or the environment. Some examples we look at include how people use social power, technology, or policy to bring about some desired end.

Part III: Assessing Capabilities looks at how your judgment influences the development of abilities, like habits, skills, and expertise, and how your assessment of your own capabilities influences your thinking and life decisions. *Chapter 5: The Human Condition* looks at how a person's overall condition improves or declines as a result of physical or intellectual development. For example, skills development can improve your mental condition when it helps you to build self-confidence. *Chapter 6: Skills Development* focuses on how you can improve your condition, or change your behavior, as a result of developing new skills. Doing that not only improves your fitness for performing life roles, but also your ability to achieve goals.

Part IV: Assessing Motives looks at how your ability to assess your own motives, or that of other people's, can influence your ability to motivate behavior toward achieving goals. In *Chapter 7: A Theory of Motivation* we look at how people are primarily motivated by their own interests to make gains and avoid losses, in terms of the things they want. This chapter also looks at other aspects of motivation, like value creation, or why people are motivated to seek justice. *Chapter 8: Motivating Productivity* looks at how to increase personal productivity by using various techniques, like incentives, goal setting, or encouragement. And *Chapter*

9: Motivating Cooperation looks at what it means to have a healthy relationship, how to strengthen a relationship by improving trust and confidence, and how to keep a relationship stable by reducing conflict.

And lastly, *Part V: Assessing Stress & Adversity* looks at how human judgment influences stress levels. People sometimes make decisions that increase unnecessary distress, which can have a negative influence on the decisions they make. In *Chapter 10: Stress Management,* we look at different forms of stress, how stress impairs judgment and leads to terrible decisions, and techniques for managing stress. And *Chapter 11: Mental Health* explores the effects of adversity on mental health, and how adversity can be caused by poor judgment.

Adversity creates distress. And, in its more severe forms, it can cause serious harm or prevent healthy growth and development. Educating people about different forms of adversity and the harm they cause, whether it is created by social biases, racial biases, child abuse or neglect, social isolation, bullying, and other forms, may help to reduce adversity.

Understanding these positive and negative influences on the human condition can make it easier to engineer more effective developmental programs for reducing social problems. For example, reducing social problems, like mass shootings, can be complicated because it involves reducing the harmful influences on the human condition, like adversity. And it involves increasing positive influences, like pursuing goals, having a life purpose, and skills development. Decreasing adversity and developing capabilities makes for a state-of-mind that is more self-confident and resilient. When people face a lot of adversity and lack well-defined goals they are actively working toward, they are less-likely to have a positive outlook on life, and more likely to fight-back or give-up in the face of difficulties.

While this book contains, and is based on, research, some which is used in previous works, it's not meant to be merely a research project. At a top level, it was developed to be a practical, science-based, system for analyzing, and forming, judgments to solve human problems. It can help private individuals make better decisions and more effectively guide their own development. And it can enable scientists and researchers to develop better programs, and solve complex social problems.

Without new theories to research, Scientists don't make progress. And this book is part theoretical science, which includes my own theories based on what the science suggests. And it is part practical science in that the topics contained in this book can be used in everyday life and in business management, to improve real-world, objective, results. In fact, if my own experience has not shown me how a topic presented in this book applies in practice, it did not get included. A tremendous amount of thought and effort went into basing my research on universal human attributes to create studies that are reproducible. To that end, this book draws from diverse fields of study, including psychology, business, technology, theoretical science, and my own life experiences.

Disclaimer: This book is not meant to provide advice about mental health. Mental health problems have many causes, including infections, tumors, chemistry, and many other causes, that need to be diagnosed by one or more qualified mental health professionals.

PART I:
ASSESSING JUDGMENT

From ancient wisdom to modern science, spiritual leaders, political leaders, and scientific geniuses, have all sought enlightenment to discover the secrets of wisdom in their judgment and decision-making. And for good reason. Human judgment shapes our world in many profound ways that people often don't understand. And this book looks at some of the core critical abilities of human judgment that shapes people's lives, along with their successes and failures.

Your judgment truly goes to the core of your behavior as it applies to how you think about yourself, other people, and the world around you. Every choice you make, and every action you perform, depends on your judgment to assess the best course of action. Your brain has to make many types of judgments to navigate the world and determine what you need to do. To do that, your judgment relies on a number of abilities, like recognition, spatial relationships, scheduling, and productivity, all to achieve your desired ends. These complex and interdependent abilities work together, like the cogs and gears of a machine, to speculate about unknowns, predict consequences, estimate time, measure quantities, interpret circumstances and people's intentions, assess threats, and many other capabilities that enable you to make decisions about what to do.

Critical thinking skills are skills that enable you to exercise better judgment. You rely on many different forms of judgment when making decisions, and have different reasons for why you make mistakes. But one of the more common causes of errors and mistakes that we look at in this book is uncertainty caused by missing, or insufficient, information. Intuitively, it makes since that to reduce uncertainty, all you need to do is get more information. But the techniques for acquiring that information may not be as direct and intuitive as it may seem. For example, you may need to quantify data, or collect information from more credible sources, rather than believing gossip.

Each part of this book could be considered a critical thinking skill. These thinking skills don't simply involve thinking critically about other people's choices and decisions, they involve thinking critically about your own decisions to avoid making serious mistakes when you need to. This ability to assess your own judgment, could be called your metacritique, or your ability to judge your own judgment. Metacritical thinking skills include your ability to spot poor judgment and know how to use better judgment when you need to.

The fundamental problem of judgment that this book addresses is not that people are imperfect and make mistakes. Intuition is your default mode of thinking. And so, you will speculate, make guesses, and bet on outcomes. Sometimes you will be right. Other times you won't. But what is important is not that you are capable of avoiding mistakes, but that you know how to spot poor judgment, and exercise better judgment when it matters.

Critical decisions tend to be high-risk or high-impact decisions, often made in your occupation or career. These are decisions that you will likely be judged or criticized for, or what some call *character defining moments*. Most daily decisions tend to be very low-risk, low-impact, decisions. No one cares if you forgot to wash your dishes before you left for work. That's a negligible and inconsequential mistake. But a decision that could that do significant harm, cause serious damage, or cause unnecessary distress, can quickly become a recognizable problem, and would be considered a critical decision.

Currently, people are not taught how to use better judgment. And because of that, their decisions tend to be heavily influenced by beliefs, biases, and peers. In many instances, education can improve judgment. In fact, the whole purpose of college education, and expertise in general, is to help the professional to predict, and understand, the consequences of different types of decisions. For example, what happens when a Brain Surgeon cuts into a specific part of the brain? Or what happens when a Construction Engineer fails to use enough concrete in the foundation of a building? People with the right training know the answers to these questions and is why they can use better judgment when making those decisions.

Completely avoiding mistakes in your decision-making may never be possible. But you can certainly improve your judgment to reduce those mistakes. The problem is, no one is born with critical thinking skills; they have to be developed with effort and practice. And whether people, in general, learn the topics in this book is mostly a wish and a hope. Many people can, and do, intuitively learn many of these skills as they age. But they still rely on good luck and fortune to have the right random experiences, social influences, education, and upbringing, to develop many of these skills.

What often happens is that people mirror the thinking habits, biases, and wrong assumptions, of their peers and social influences as they stive for acceptance. Whether a person ever develops these skills at all, can never be known for certain. We only know of the negative consequences of not having them. And telling a person to use good judgment, or behave responsibly, may not help when that person has no idea what you mean. Or worse, the person gets offended because it is seen as an attack on one's character or intelligence.

Scientists and educators have long known these problems exist, and need to be dealt with. Educators create programs to inform students on miscellaneous topics, like the perils of substance use, racial biases, teen pregnancies, cyberbullying, or how to become an effective leader, from grades five through twelve. All of these are common situations where people sometimes use bad judgment that require critical thinking skills to navigate. Maybe, one day, with better theories, better research, and greater enlightenment, we can finally begin to forge a path to better judgment.

1

Good Judgment

Historically, ideas about what constitutes good judgment is a subject of debate. So, it's helpful to briefly look at what other researchers have concluded about what constitutes good judgment. In 2020, Sir Andrew Likierman published an article in the Harvard Business Review entitled the *Elements of Good Judgment: How to improve your decision-making*. In his article, Likierman does a great job of drawing from insight and observations about human judgment from leaders of all walks of life, including CEOs of startups, CEOs of global enterprises, senior partners, doctors, scientists, and other professionals. In his article, he uses their insight to identify the skills and behaviors that enable leaders to recognize patterns that other people miss.

According to Likierman's research, the ability to listen is among the many traits that enable leaders to exercise better judgment. Leaders who appear to have good judgment are great listeners, learners, and readers. They try to recognize how their own biases influence their judgment, including their ability to process information and learn from experience. By excluding their own biases, they do a better job at paying attention to what people actually mean and are able to "understand, clarify, and accept different viewpoints."

Leaders who exercise good judgment not only consider the facts, data, and evidence to make data-driven decisions, they also make judgment calls based on their own life experiences, drawing from their knowledge of what works, or does not work. Anytime they don't know something, they rely on the judgment of people who do, like professionals or experts on the subject. They are capable of drawing on the skills and experiences of trusted advisors, who don't necessarily echo or validate their own ideas. Good judgment, he says, results from being able to turn knowledge into understanding. And people fail to do that, according to Likierman, because they filter out a considerable amount of information they disagree with, or are not critical enough of the information they receive.

Leaders who use good judgment also tend to question the solution and expand on the choices under consideration. When people fail to consider all their options, they are more likely to make decisions that have unintended consequences. When more options can be presented and debated, it allows teams to arrive at better solutions. And ideally those options should identify key facts and risks, and how those risks will be mitigated using modeling, testing, or computer aided technologies, to reduce the chances of unintended consequences. Leaders with strong judgment also consider the potential real-world consequences of their decisions. By anticipating risks associated with implementing a solution, and trying to understand its feasibility, they improve their odds of delivering the proposed solution.

At the end of the article, Likierman closes with the statement: "Those with ambition but no judgment run out of money. Those with charisma but no judgment lead their followers in the wrong direction. Those with passion but no judgment hurl themselves down the wrong paths. Those with drive but no judgment get up very early to do the wrong things. Sheer luck and factors beyond your control may determine your eventual success, but good judgment will stack the cards in your favor."[33]

Likierman's conclusions may be absolutely correct. But to understand why, we have to take a slightly deeper dive into the underlying science that could explain why his conclusions may be correct, in addition to how much further the subject of human judgment can be developed. And that is exactly what we will begin doing in the next chapter.

CHAPTER 1:
COGNITIVE LIMITATIONS

In ancient history, Socrates was regarded as one of the wisest people of his time. Much of his philosophy, according to his student Plato, concerned matters of knowledge. He would constantly question what people think they know. And in several recorded statements, he suggested that people become wiser as they acquire insight into how little they really know about the world, an idea that was later called the *Socratic Paradox*. In 399BC, Socrates was sentenced to death for "corrupting the minds of the youth."[37]

So, why do ideas like the Socratic Paradox survive the ages, rather than being forgotten or replaced by more modern philosophical ideas? The answer to that question is in the fundamental problem of human judgment. And that is, people do not understand the world, or how it works, as well as they intuitively believe they do. If people where all-knowing, omniscient, beings who knew everything, they would never make mistakes because they would always be able to predict the consequences of any decision. But people form wrong conclusions about how their world works all the time, yet they are convinced they are correct.

Being a skilled critic not only involves thinking critically about the people around you, it involves thinking critically about your own abilities, weaknesses, and areas in which you need improvement. In this chapter, we look at limitations in cognitive abilities that constrain your ability to know about the world and how it works. And we look at how those limitations cause people to make mistakes in their judgment.

The inability to recognize these human limitations is, in itself, a weakness that perpetuates more bad judgment and more bad decisions. So, we will start with a very brief introduction to the subject of mental models and will continue to progress into the biological reasons those models are constrained. And in the next chapter, we look at some techniques for overcoming those limitations by relying on better, more accurate, models of reality.

1

Mental Models

When you make a judgment, your judgment is not entirely based on reality, but instead on a mental representation of reality. Any mental representation, whether it consists of memories of life experiences, dreams, imaginary creations, thoughts, concepts, ideas, or theories, are all mental models or mental simulations. In fact, human expression, language, story-telling, and mathematical computations, would not be possible without the brain's ability to store these mental representations. Collectively, they make-up your world model, or world view, which is your unique perspective of the world and how it works. As you age and learn more about the world, your mental models evolve, develop, and become more complex, and hopefully more informed over-time.

Your mental models also contain values and knowledge

that inform your judgment. Your *values* include things that you want, and value more highly than others, that often have benefit and usefulness in your pursuits. On a personal level, they define your unique interests, preferences, and opinions. And on a social level, they may include friends, family, professional skills, or material items. Some of your values are unique to you, and some you share with others.

When you judge the world around you, including other people's decisions, you tend to evaluate those things based on your own values. Anything that is valued, is wanted. And anything that is not valued, is not wanted. This type of estimation, often called a *value-based judgment*, guides many of your choices and decisions.

Forming judgments based on what you value and want may be quick and easy, but forming judgments based on truthful and accurate information is a little more difficult. These types of judgments are *knowledge-based judgments*, in which the truth can be known, but may not be known for certain. For example, if you know little about something, you may speculate, form beliefs, and make assumptions about it, which may cause you to make errors and mistakes in judgment. These errors occur because of missing, or insufficient, information needed to arrive at a correct conclusion. These types of judgments are integral to the pursuit of values because knowledge is the means, or the *know-how*, by which you obtain more of what you want. Because of this, problems in making knowledge-based judgments are going to cause problems in bringing about desired consequences.

Anytime you are faced with uncertainty and you form a judgment based on what you already know, e.g., a few superficial details, that judgment will be fast, easy, and intuitive. But, as we've already seen, doing that also leads to mistakes. If you make a decision based on incomplete information, you may be missing a key detail that could completely change your choice from one option to another. In these circumstances, improving your judgment requires additional thinking and effort to obtain more information. And that effort can certainly pay-off with better consequences, especially when making important or critical decisions.

This goes to the core of why some experts are said to have better acumen. Some sports coaches, for example, are said to have better sports acumen, not because they have better judgment in general, but because they know enough about their subject to be successful. Rather than merely speculating about what works, as many non-professionals would, they have a repository of expertise, experience, and real-world examples, to draw from about what is proven to work in reality. They have the know-how to produce objective results, so they are not relying entirely on subjective beliefs. But while it takes a considerable amount of time and effort to build more accurate and reliable mental models, doing so results in better judgment and better decisions.

2

Cognitive Limitations

The central problem of human judgment, and the quality of mental models in general, is one of cognitive limitations. To overcome those limitations and improve your judgment, you have to be aware of your cognitive deficits. In the previous section, we looked at how one of those deficits involves knowledge, and how people tend to have an incomplete, or inaccurate, knowledge the world around them. But biological limitations also create many of our cognitive deficits.

The human brain can only store a small amount of information about objective reality upon which to make decisions. When you observe a physical object, you see a superficial representation constructed by your nervous system. You can speculate about the materials that make-up that object. But you may not know anything about its chemical composition, where it was made, or where it came from. These gaps in intelligence, force you to make guesses, make assumptions, and make predictions based on probabilities, which inevitably leads to errors and mistakes.

In the following sections, we look at the biological limitations that cause people to make mistakes, starting with the brain's executive ability. Other cognitive limitations include the brain's ability to accurately store and recall memory, reliance on intuition, and emotions that exaggerate memories and distort judgment. All of these cause people to make regrettable mistakes. And, in many cases, these mental faculties may be improved.

3
Executive Ability

Similar to how a Chief Executive Officer (CEO) for a corporation executes strategies to achieve corporate goals, you are the CEO of your own life and personal business. You make executive decisions about what to do, what goals to pursue, and what to avoid. *Executive ability* is your brain's ability to execute strategies and achieve goals.

Human behavior, as we will see throughout this book, is highly goal oriented as people are motivated to pursue their own interests. Those interests could include anything, from your basic, existential, needs for food and safety, to more complex social and financial goals. As you pursue those goals, your brain is constantly responding to opportunities and threats, seeking to make wanted gains and trying to defend your interests. Executive ability is the mental faculty that governs these responses and makes decisions about what to do.

Executive ability is believed to be governed by a part of the brain called the Prefrontal Cortex, which controls time management, planning and scheduling, strategy, problem solving, social behaviors, cognitive focus, and other goal-oriented behaviors. While the entire brain may be used when forming judgments, the Prefrontal Cortex may play the most dominant role in human judgment. As your brain takes in sensory input, and the executive part of the brain processes and interprets that input, it makes decisions about what to do. A different part of the brain, the Limbic System, which is the emotional and impulsive part of the brain, also influences decision-making and, sometimes, more than the Prefrontal Cortex.

Research by Neuroscientists has found that reduced functionality in the Prefrontal Cortex can impair judgment and lead to poor decisions. In fact, an adolescent Prefrontal Cortex that is not yet fully developed, according to Neuroscientist B. J. Casey in a National Public Radio story, is more likely to uninhibitedly fight threats and pursue opportunities, which can result in poor decisions. In other words, the Prefrontal Cortex plays a central role in restraining the emotional part of the brain with logic and reason, according to Casey.[54]

Neuroscientists Antonio Damasio and his colleagues, have also studied people with damage in the Prefrontal Cortex, and in the emotional centers of the brain, and found

they have substantially reduced motivation, poor judgment, and tend to exhibit socially inappropriate behaviors.[41]

Some age-related conditions, like Alzheimer's disease,
can cause memory loss and deterioration in parts of the
brain, including the Prefrontal Cortex in later stages, which
results in poor judgment. People with Alzheimer's may
have difficulty predicting the consequences of behavior,
like wandering into a busy street during rush hour, or giving money to strangers. In some cases, they have problems
with grooming and hygiene, dressing appropriately for the
given weather conditions, or difficulty judging distance
while driving.[22]

And many other conditions reduce activity in the Prefrontal Cortex and impair judgment. Some of those include
chemical intoxication, sleep deprivation, excessive stress,
emotional disturbances, a lack of healthy nutrition, and a
lack of physical and mental exercise. Toxins, like alcohol
consumption, not only reduce activity in the Prefrontal Cortex, it can impair judgment by causing reduced comprehension, poor coordination, difficulty concentrating, and
memory problems. According to the U.S. Department of
Health and Human Services, the impaired judgment caused
by substance use leads to drownings, crimes, imprisonment, and death, and leads to hospital bills from emergency
room visits, long-term healthcare costs, and rehabilitation
costs.[11]

Improving executive function is certainly possible. Since
the brain is, after all, an organ that is part of the physical
body, healthy nutrition can improve brain and body composition, and physical exercise can increase blood flow, oxygen, and nutrients to the brain. Even learning, and forming
new memories, can stimulate the brain's neurogenerative

abilities and improve memory, attention, and comprehension. And developing new skills with practice and exercise can improve executive ability by improving your ability to perform a role.

4

Memory

The mental models that make-up your life experiences are stored in memory, which is not the most reliable or accurate storage medium. The problem with human memory is that recalling, or reconstructing, onetime events in great detail can be problematic. It's problematic because it depends on your focus of attention and the amount of detail you observe and remember.

Research by Elizabeth Loftus has found that people sometimes fill-in missing details to account for unknowns in a way that seems logical and plausible, but can create false memories. During the mid-1970s, Loftus and her colleagues conducted a series of studies to explore the occurrence of false memories.[35] In one of her studies, 100 students were asked about a film featuring a multi-car accident. Each student was asked questions about events that occurred in the film, or events that did not occur in the film. For example, some questions were worded: "Did you see the _____?" which suggests that the subject did appear in the film. And others were worded: "Did you see a _____?" which suggests that the subject may not have appeared in the film. Respondents were more likely to say that they saw the subject when the question implied it appeared in the film.

What this research suggests is that when people reconstruct events from memory, they sometimes accept a plausible version of reality, even when those events never happened, thus creating a false memory. And this, as Loftus pointed out, can be especially problematic in criminal trials. When police and prosecutors try to build a case against a defendant, they may be basing that case on a plausible scenario. And when an eye witness is unable to remember the event accurately, that witness may accept the plausible version and may, inadvertently, give false testimony.

Exercising good judgment, requires the ability to distinguish between strong and weak memories and either ignore weak memories, or seek-out the truth. Weak memories are notorious for being inaccurate and can, unwittingly, lead to regrettable lies and mistakes. Developing strong memory requires attention, cognitive focus, and reflection. This is similar to an actor learning the lines of a play and, with practice, reciting those lines with increasing accuracy. Anytime you are uncertain, or are confronted with a disagreement about the factuality or truthfulness of a statement, you can fact-check your knowledge and correct yourself.

In a later chapter on skills development, we look at how the mind is like a muscle in that the more you flex an ability, the stronger that ability becomes. The more you try to remember something, the stronger that memory gets. These mind-building exercises not only help you build strong memories, they can make you more mentally fit and productive in performing a role.

Improving the accuracy and completeness of memory can also create a more accurate representation of reality, which can improve problem solving and predictive abilities. The more frequently you perform a task, like commuting to work, the more information you acquire. More information allows you to see patterns that can improve your ability to predict future outcomes. In your morning commute, for example, you can better recognize places where slow-downs occur and learn faster routes. In this way, creating better memories can improve the accuracy of your mental models, which can allow you to make better decisions.

5
Emotions

Your judgment and decision-making are highly influenced by emotions. If you are unhappy about something in your life, it can motivate you to make a positive change. Excitement about an upcoming event can motivate you to prepare for that event. Love, as an emotion, can bind couples together, which make them closer and more committed to helping one another.

Research has also shown that emotions may influence the strength of memories. While most people do not remember most daily events in great detail, significant life-changing events that are highly emotional, like the birth of a child or a terrorist attack, may be recalled more vividly. These are usually profound world-changing events that people reflect on, think about, talk about, and try to explain, which creates a better mental record of the event.

But emotions, especially when they are triggered by distress, can be detrimental to good judgment and can lead to poor, and impulsive, decisions that are out-of-character and have harmful consequences. Emotions tend to exaggerate the way people judge others, making them much better or worse than they really are. Emotions, like extreme anger or sadness, can also exaggerate the severity of events. A person with depression may increasingly become inconsolably sad to the point of giving-up. Anger can motivate a person to lie about others, make verbally abusive and dehumanizing comments, punch a hole in the wall, or do other things that are typically out of character.

As people recall their lives, they tend to create a life narrative, internal dialog, or self-talk, which is the story a person tells oneself to make since out of life. This self-talk can positively or negatively influence one's emotional state. For example, suppose Tina is always angry at her boss for being a jerk. When Tina continues to tell herself that her boss is a jerk, and harbors resentment about him, she's creating a reason to be angry about her life situation. And those problems can become generalized so that a few terrible life experiences can appear worse and more wide-spread than they really are. Not only is her boss a jerk, but her previous boyfriend whom she broke up with is also a jerk, so all men must be jerks. This mental model may not accurately represent reality. And Tina really needs to look beyond those events to create a better life narrative.

6
Intuition

When you interact with the world around you, you are speculating about, and figuring out, the world based on previous experiences. Sometimes you will be right. And other times you will make mistakes. This speculative way of interacting with your environment is called intuition, or gut-instinct. Intuition is your default mode of thinking, primarily because it requires the least amount of effort. Any time you try to understand, and make sense out of, the world around you based on your observations and what you already know, you are using intuition.

For most daily decisions, like what to wear for the day, or what to eat for lunch, intuition has the advantage of allowing you to make quick and easy decisions without getting bogged down by the details. You don't need to do extensive online research, or consult with an expert, to know whether a vegetable is good to eat. All you need is a little common sense to see, smell, and taste the vegetable. These are low-risk, low-impact, decisions that have minor and inconsequential outcomes.

Intuition actually plays important role in decision-making in that it can often point you in the right direction, and sometimes to the correct conclusion. But intuition alone does not always lead to correct conclusions. Intuition is like the speculative part of decision-making that allows you to intuitively make guesses and form conclusions about your world, similar to how a scientist forms a hypothesis about some natural phenomenon. But even the scientist has to do more research, and conduct more experiments, to know whether a hypothesis has merit. So, while intuition is helpful for pointing you in the right direction, judgment tends to be better when it is based on known and provable facts, rather than intuition or beliefs. And that's especially true if you need to make a calculated decision that may impact people's lives.

Psychologists Amos Tversky and Daniel Kahneman, who are famed for their research on how the brain processes information when faced with uncertainty, found that people tend to use heuristics, which are like intuitive rules of thumb that guide people in their decision-making. An example of using a heuristic would be choosing a known brand you are familiar with at the super market so you are not left dissatisfied with your choice.

Tversky and Kahneman also demonstrated how intuition tends to result in cognitive biases, in which people are inclined to favor one thing over another. Biases, when it comes to knowledge-based decisions, often do result in poor judgment. The problem is, when a person makes a decision based on a bias, that person usually does not take into account enough information to arrive at a correct conclusion. When making low-risk decisions, like what t-shirt to buy, biases are not a problem. But when making a judgment about a defendant's guilt in a criminal case without sufficient evidence, it could certainly do serious harm if the defendant is truly innocent.

Bias training can be a way to improve judgment for specific problems, like racial biases. But bias training, alone, only goes so far to inform people about the problems of bad judgment. For example, it does not address the central problem of bad judgment, which is almost always rooted in missing, or insufficient, information. And this applies to cognitive biases as well. When a person has a racial bias, for example, that person is forming a pre-judgment purely based on race, while discarding all other important information about the person.

When you form a judgment based on your intuition, you are directly relying on your mental representation of the world and how it works. And that directly influences your beliefs. Your beliefs about what is true or not, or what is probable, is largely based on your world model and life experiences. In other words, if a statement does not match your mental model of the way something works, you may be inclined to disbelieve it. And that, by itself, can create a weakness in judgment because you cannot always know for certain whether your mental models of reality are correct, since they could be based on faulty, or incomplete, memories. For that reason, intuition is not always the most trustworthy and reliable source of truth. And you may need a more reliable source of information when trying to form a more accurate and truthful judgment.

7

Mental Logic

When people intuitively form judgments, or make decisions, they tend to form logical conclusions based on mental models of how reality works. For example, if a person is in a terrible situation, then that person must have done something terrible to deserve it. Or if a restaurant does not have much business, then they must have terrible food. A person may believe that the world works this way, but all of these conclusions could be completely wrong because they are entirely based, not on reality, but on that person's mental logic.

Interestingly, these logical arguments can also be a way to test the soundness of a person's judgment by testing the mental logic upon which that judgment is made. Consider the fact that mental logic tends to follow a pattern similar to propositional statements. For example, if some condition (x) is true, then condition (y) must also be true. Or, if condition (x), then do condition (y). If your brain receives a signal that your body is hungry, then respond by executing "if hungry, then eat" which mobilizes you to eat. Or, if the proposition "the weather is too cold" is true, then stay inside.

Computer technologies operate using similar logic, except rather than basing operational logic on mental models comprise of sensory input, their logic is based on data models comprised of binary data. When writing programs, software developers use propositional statements to guide a program's behavior. Those "flow control" statements include logic, like if-then-else statements, while loops, for-each loops, and other types of decisions statements that are triggered by various conditions. How those statements are arranged together to perform some function is called an algorithm. And developers can design algorithms by using a variety of modelling techniques, like flow charts, Unified Modeling Language (UML) diagrams, and other modeling methods.

Human intelligence uses a similar type of instruction set. You probably recognize that certain conditions must be met to achieve specific goals. For example, if you do not study, you will fail the exam. Or, if the time is 10pm, then go to bed, else watch the news. While the time is between 10pm and 6am, sleep. For each page in the book, read to end. This type of conditional logic, or decisions based on specific conditions, also dictates the rules people live by including their principles, values, and preferences. You may schedule time, plan the day, and program a series of activities, to help you achieve specific ends. Or, if you want to stay fit, then create an exercise regimen for engaging in physical activity a few days a week. People establish these routines and procedural logic as a way of programming their lives to make complicated decisions easier and more automatic.

8
Logical Errors

Anytime you form a logical conclusion about the world based on a mental model, that model may not contain enough information to arrive at a correct conclusion. And when it doesn't, the result is a logic error, or bad logic, which is a mistake in how the brain processes information. Errors and mistakes occur for many reasons. But the most common reason when making a knowledge-based decision is missing information.

That is especially true when forming a judgment about something you are seeing for the first time and know little about. In these circumstances, it's easy to form a judgment, only to admit later you didn't know a key piece of information that would have changed your judgment. This can cause problems when people fail to recognize their error, and continue to act on bad logic anyway.

Data models have a similar problem. But the way application developers handle the problem of missing, or insufficient, information, is with additional validation logic. For example, suppose an application developer writes a program for a grade school classroom that requires students to enter their information. A valid age in the system may be between 1 and 100. If a student fails to enter an age, the application displays a message telling the student to enter an age. That, of course, does not guarantee that all the information is correct. If a student meant to enter an age of 6, but enters the age of 66, it passes the program's validation check. If the instructor verifies the entries, she will discover the discrepancy and can fix it. People are like computers, in a way, in that they need error checking encoded into them to prevent these types of logical blunders.

Another type of error occurs when a model infers that some condition (y) exclusively depends on condition (x), when the two have no relationship. For example, if Susan left her job, then she must have performed poorly. Or one could further conclude that if Susan performed her job well, then her employer would want her to stay and would promote her. Both of these conclusions could be false because the real reason she left may have nothing to do with how well she performed.

Part of the reason this logic is so convincing is that it is partially based in reality, even when the logic itself is untrue. For example, consider the statement: "if you work hard, you will be financially successful." An obvious problem with this statement is that you could work hard and end-up with nothing, especially if you are not getting paid for all of your work. But since work is what employers pay for, it logically makes since that the more you work, the more money you should earn.

Again, this error is rooted in insufficient information because we really don't know the reason why the person is not financially successful. We would have to do addition work to find out the truth. So, the statement "I don't know why he's not financially successful" is a true statement. And since you cannot know everything, you are not going to get yourself into trouble with that admission. But the statement "he is not financially successful because he is lazy and doesn't want to work," may not necessarily true and may cause unfair discrimination during a hiring decision.

You can find other, similar, forms of faulty logic that can lead people down very dark paths. For example, consider what some Psychologists call the Gambler's Fallacy, in which a person thinks that future probabilities are altered by past events. A gambler may not know the outcome of a bet, but he knows that he must gamble to win. And that remains true, even when he continues losing all of his money while remaining biasly optimistic he will eventually win it back.[27]

This type of logic can be encouraging and beneficial, but

it can also be discouraging and harmful. If you are operating under the assumption, "if I work hard, I will be financially successful" that logic can be encouraging and beneficial. But if you are operating under the assumption "I got fired, so no one will want to hire me" then that statement would be discouraging and could cause more harm than good.

People who leave their former employer, even if it was on bad terms, can sometimes find better, higher paying, employment. And of course, you can find many other examples in which faulty logic causes harm. For example, when an innocent person is convicted of a crime, or an employee is fired over a misunderstanding, or a political leader creates a law that has unintended consequences. Those people are not necessarily evil, diabolical, people. They may think they are making the right decisions, but are ignorant of the consequences.

9

Critical Skills

To strengthen your judgment when making critical decisions, you have to question your judgment and consider the possibility that you may be wrong. People have considerable limitations in their cognitive abilities that often lead to errors in thinking and mistakes. Facts are sometimes remembered incorrectly. Or ideas that appear to be wrong may actually turn out to be correct. So, unless you are an expert and have a good solid understanding of a subject, you cannot always rely on your knowledge, and your recollection of events, to make the best judgment.

The less you trust your own knowledge when making the most critical decisions, the more motivated you may be to find the right answers. That, of course, does not necessarily have to mean you don't value, or have confidence in, your abilities. It simply acknowledges that you could be wrong about this one critical decision, and you may have to expend extra effort to find out the truth.

Executive ability, or the brain's executive function, may play an important role in your self-awareness of these cognitive limitations. In theory, we could speculate that when the executive part of the brain is highly functional, a person who is trained to recognize one's own cognitive weaknesses, may recognize those weaknesses quicker than someone who has a low functioning Prefrontal Cortex. And a person with reduced executive ability, especially someone who is not trained to recognize one's weaknesses, may be more likely to form wrong conclusions and act on those conclusions. That, of course, is pure theory and speculation.

When making critical decisions, you also need to be aware of how your emotions can influence your judgment. When people are emotional, things may appear better, or worse, than they really are. And because of that, your emotions do not provide the most accurate assessment of your circumstances, especially in distressing situations. If you get too caught-up in what you are doing emotionally, it can motivate behavior that you will later regret.

You should also avoid making critical decisions purely based on intuition, and intuitive logic. Your intuition can be invaluable for pointing you in the right direction. But it does not necessarily lead to correct conclusions. Intuitive logic, like "if a restaurant does not have many customers, their food must be terrible" is not necessarily a correct or factual statement. In that instance, you should question your own judgment because to really know, you have to dine there.

In the next chapter, we look at how to overcome cognitive limitations by developing the intellectual skills that improve the accuracy of judgment, in the same way an archer improves the accuracy of his shot. Some of that requires adopting new ways of thinking that emerged during the Scientific Revolution, when people began to realize that reality, as they perceive it, cannot be unintuitively understood. This thinking led to the creation of a systematic process that is, today, called Science, by which people attempt to test and deconstruct natural phenomena to understand how it works. We also look at modeling techniques that not only improve the accuracy of your models, but improve the decisions you make.

CHAPTER 2:
RESEARCH METHODS

The last chapter looked at how poor judgment is often caused by natural biological limitations and missing information. You could consider this a person's natural state of ignorance. The path to enlightenment, requires you to step out of the darkness of ignorance and into the light of knowledge. And to do that when making a critical decision, you have to follow practices that enable you to fill-in those missing details with quality information. The better quality of information, the greater certainty you will have in your decision-making.

This chapter explores some examples of effective research methods for extracting the information required to improve certainty in decision-making. Some types and sources of information are better than others. And when you recognize a lack of knowledge and try to fill-in that knowledge, it's important that your information comes from a reputable source that is truthful, accurate, and unbiased. Failing to do that, not only leads to wrong conclusions, but poor decisions and unintended consequences.

1
Choices

The first step in any decision-making process involves evaluating your choices. Anytime you have more than one option or opportunity, you have a *choice*. And you use your judgment to make the best choice among alternatives.

Choices that have more desirable outcomes tend to make for better decisions. If a choice would result in a positive consequence for yourself and others, others may agree that you made a good decision. But if a choice results in a negative consequence, especially when other people are negatively impacted by it, others may agree that you made a poor decision.

Every day of your life is like a new blank canvas. And just as a painter has a choice about what brushstroke to put on the canvas, you have a choice about what to do for the day. You may have already made some of those choices based on your life goals. You may have career goals, or financial goals, and strive to achieve those by building a business or working for an employer.

The problem with the idea that life is a product of choices is that you can only make choices about things that are within your sphere of control. You don't have a choice about where you were born, your genetics, the forces of nature, the passage of time, financial disparities, or disabilities. So, you cannot choose to be anything, like the President of the United States, a beautiful fashion model, or a famous entertainer, unless you believe you can compete for those positions.

But people are also not completely helpless and at the mercy of the circumstance, either. You have a choice about your own personal development, skills development, and improving your mental and physical fitness. Yet, you are undeniably constrained by time, money, and other resources, in striving to achieve your goals.

Economist Herbert Simon once pointed out that the problem with choosing is that people have bounded rationality, in which they are limited in time, cognitive ability, and information. Because of these limitations, people are forced to accept satisfactory outcomes, rather than ideal outcomes. As people expand their options, they try to do one of two things: They choose the option that sufficiently meets their minimum requirements within the constraints of their limited means, which Simon called *satisficing*, or they choose the best option given their limited means, which we could call *optimizing*.

To understand the difference between making a sufficient and optimal choice, suppose you are considering buying a coffee table. If you only need one that is functional, you could buy an old, used, scratched-up coffee table at a garage sale. And that would be a sufficient choice. On the other hand, if you want a nicer, more expensive, coffee table that you will not quickly replace in the future, you may look for the best one among the alternatives, given your limited time and money. That would be an example of making an optimal choice.

To make the best choice, you want to start by expanding your options to see what choices are available and then choosing the sufficient or optimal option depending on your needs. But if you fail to explore your options, you are ignoring a significant amount of information, which forces you to make a less-than sufficient or optimal choice.

Suppose Frank is considering moving to a new apartment. He could simply go with his first option and, in doing so, may make a choice he later regrets. But if he expands his options, and weighs the pros and cons of living in different apartments in the surrounding area, he stands a better chance at making a decision he will be happy with in the long-term.

This scenario demonstrates how a greater number of options can lead to better decisions. But research also reveals that too many options can be overwhelming, and may cause you to make a random choice with a less-than desirable outcome. To avoid that, you need to limit, or narrow, your options to only the most desirable ones, which will make your choice easier and more intuitive. Alternatively, you can seek the advice of an expert who knows a great deal about those options and could help you make an informed decision.

In their book *Nudge: Improving Decisions About Health, Wealth, and Happiness*, Richard Thaler and Cass Sunstein, suggest that choices can be made easier by providing default options that nudge people to make better choices. For example, employers could provide a default option that automatically opts-in their employees for health insurance or retirement savings accounts. Employees would still have the option to opt-out. But providing those default options encourages employees to stick with choices they will not later regret if they need health insurance or money for retirement.[52]

2

Quality of Information

In the previous chapter, we looked at how having incomplete, or inaccurate, information usually results in poor judgment. And that is no different when making choices. Even when you have many different options, knowing very little about those options, or having bad information about them, will not help you make the best choice.

Quality of information (QoI) refers to the completeness, and accuracy, of information. And when making critical decisions, you want the highest QoI to inform your judgment. Higher QoI tends to reduce uncertainty about what choices result in better outcomes. In the following sections, we look at some techniques for improving the quality of the information.

3

Subjective Experience vs. Objective Reality

When you make a judgment, your judgment may be based on subjective experience, like beliefs, emotions, or opinions. Or, it could be based on objective reality, which includes the reality that exists beyond human perception. Many philosophers, like George Berkley in his book published in 1710, entitled a *Treatise Concerning the Principles of Human Knowledge,* argued that all reality is subjective since people can only view it through the lens of human perception. But people have devised methods for testing objective reality to determine whether their conclusions are correct. And today, we call these techniques Science.

The fact that human reality is viewed through the lens of human perception, creates a paradoxical problem in which people often have difficulty distinguishing between subjective experience and objective reality, which leads to poor judgment. For example, people often try to solve their problems, and figure things out, intuitively, which relies heavily on subjective mental models. In most cases, that is not a problem. But when making critical decisions, relying on what you already know may not be enough to improve the objective consequences.

Relying on intuition is desirable because it only requires a small amount of effort. But it's also highly error prone. Unless you are an expert in an advanced subject, like performing brain surgery, then forming a judgment about what to do based on first impressions can be highly subjective and problematic since you don't have enough information to make an educated judgment.

Good intentions and wishful thinking don't go very far in bringing about a desired result. Anyone could predict, based on their own subjective experiences, that a specific course of action will lead to a specific outcome. But without enough information about the potential consequences, the real-world consequences are unknown. Public policy is an example in which intentions are sometimes used to justify negative consequences. It's nearly impossible to truly understand the full impact that policies have on private individuals, businesses, or organizations. To mitigate that damage, policy makers would need to do more research, like an impact assessment, to uncover those facts.

Another problem that occurs when people base their judgment on intuition and subjective experience, is that they are often basing their judgment on beliefs and believability. Whether something is believable only depends on how closely it matches your mental model of the world and how it works. And because of that, beliefs and believability can be easily exploited for criminal gain. Criminals only need to be believable enough to persuade their unsuspecting victims. If a good Samaritan were trying to help you, on other hand, and you found that person unbelievable, then your disbelief would only make you worse off.

You are not forced to base your judgment on beliefs or believability. You also have the faculty of knowledge and knowing or not knowing. Certainty in decision-making increases when decisions are based on knowledge and facts, which tends to be closer to objective reality, than beliefs about subjective experience. And later in this chapter, we look other techniques for improving the ability to make knowledge-based decisions.

At some point in history, people realized that nature cannot be intuitively understood from subjective experience. So, they created a systematic process for testing objective reality to determine what is true, and what is not true, which we call the Scientific Method. When applying the Scientific Method, the Scientist starts with a hypothesis, which is basically an unproven model of how nature works, and then tests that model to prove or disprove the hypothesis. When a hypothesis is proven correct, it becomes an agreed upon scientific model of nature that can be further tested, challenged, and explored by other scientists, to create a more accurate written model of the structure, composition, and mechanical properties of nature.

For most people, intuition plays a similar role to that of the hypothesis in the Scientific Method. You need to test your intuition to prove or disprove your conclusions. Only then will you know you are correct. Later in this chapter, we look at some ways of testing, and improving certainty in, the validity of your conclusions. This may seem like a lot of work. But for critical decisions that could seriously impact people's lives, doing that additional work is absolutely worth it.

4

Gossip

People are highly influenced by what they are told by other

people, including their family, friends, coworkers, or strangers online. And when you consider the quality of information provided by those sources, it raises some interesting questions. For example, how do you know who to trust and what is true? And why do people so easily believe misinformation?

Before widespread literacy, we could speculate that people's primary source of information was gossip and rumor, or what they were told by other people. Children who are not literate, almost exclusively learn about the world from family, friends, instructors, and media. So, the tendency to listen to, and believe, rumors, especially from trusted people, like friends and family, is very common even among adults.

The problem with believing rumors, is that unless the person is an expert on the subject, then what that person says is not necessarily the most credible source of information. Even the smartest, most well-educated, trustworthy, and honest people have limitations in knowledge, memory, and understanding, that causes false memories and incorrect statements. People tend to filter-out information that does not conform to their understanding of how reality works. So, they don't always tell the truth, even when they honestly believe they are telling the truth.

Added to this problem is the fact that some people lie because they have ulterior motives. Maybe they want to gain support for their efforts and causes, and will lie to get others on their side. Or they will lie about others they dislike for many reasons. The person may be a political rival, or could expose information they don't want others to hear. There is often more motivation to serve one's own self-interests than to seek out the truth, be honest, or do the right thing.

People also tend to be influenced by social pressures and ingroup biases, and reflect the views and opinions of others out of a desire for belonging. An *ingroup bias* is an inclination to favor the people and ideas of those within a social group, and have a disinclination, or dislike, of the people or ideas outside the social group. People have a desire for social acceptance because of the support it provides. And that need for acceptance, or the need to avoid rejection, causes them too cave-in to social pressures and in-group biases, to be more likable to their peers, even when doing so means believing things that are not true. That's why workers who depend on their jobs for their livelihood sometimes follow the practices of a corrupt business owner. They want to blend in and secure their position, not stick-out, go against the grain, and cause friction.

Another reason to not automatically believe gossip is that people are often terrible at fact-checking themselves, and are equally terrible at conducting investigations and doing research. From my own work experience working for employers, the few that did performance reviews always based their reviews on the word and subjective opinions of managers or workers. Or when an employee would file a report to Human Resources, HR would usually gather evidence in the form of asking employees questions and then deciding who to believe. All of these approaches are highly subjective and could easily give unscrupulous people the advantage. Managers also have other options in terms of enforcing merit systems, changing organizational structure, changing company policy, implementing well-defined objectives and metrics, and conducting tests, all of which could be more highly effective, objective, and fairer to the workforce.

Ultimately, you are responsible for your own decisions,

even if you are acting on wrong information you received from friends or strangers on the internet. For example, suppose a manager is told by an employee that a coworker is stealing from the business. In a burst of anger, the manager fires the employee. But later, the manager discovers that the suspect employee did not steal from the business. So, who is to blame? The employee who told the manager the false information, or the manager? Certainly, both are complicit to some extent. But the manager is primarily to blame for the employee's wrongful termination because the manager was responsible for investigating and fact-checking the story.

5

Studies & Research

Judgment tends to be better, and more accurate, when it is based on facts and objective reality, rather than subjective experience. And Science seeks to discover how natural phenomenon works using a systematic process of testing objective reality, collecting evidence, and validating results. A trained researcher would call this primary research. The actual process of conducting primary research and making scientific discoveries can be an expensive and time-consuming process. And most people don't have the time or resources to experiment and learn from trial-and-error mistakes the way scientists do.

So, most of us rely on secondary sources of information. These secondary sources include experts, like industry professionals or academics, who compile information from primary sources to develop new solutions or provide training. Certainly, many skeptics question whether they can trust science and the experts. And that skepticism is understandable in a market environment where some products don't do what they claim.

But Scientific research tends to be a more credible source of information, partly because Science, as a discipline, seeks the truth. But also, Science is more credible because becoming a credentialed scientist often requires extensive training and rigor. If an idea does not appear to have scientific merit, or appears to be untrue, researchers have incentive to challenge the established model, test objective reality, and find out the truth.

Since you are not going to be an expert in everything, your judgment is not going to be excellent in everything, either. Consider physical health, for example. You don't have to be a health expert to live a healthy lifestyle. But if you don't know anything about health, then you are more likely to use poor judgment when trying to maintain your physical health. So, ideally, you would listen to an expert for advice, especially one who is represented by a public health organization. And by following that advice, you can use better judgment when trying to live a healthy lifestyle.

In other words, your best friend may not provide the best advice on healthy living. But the experts, along with well-established science, can provide better advice. Learning from, and listening to, the advice of experts can help you solve problems much faster, and with less effort, than if you tried to figure it out for yourself. Rather than wasting your valuable time and energy doing trial-and-error testing, learning from mistakes, and making discoveries, the experts have already done much of that for you. And that can save you an enormous amount of time and help you to avoid those mistakes.

Experts can also make complex technical decisions easier

and more intuitive by simplifying complex factors down to a few easy choices. As an example, imagine you are looking at a seven-page wine menu, which can be overwhelming to someone, like myself, who is not a wine connoisseur. To make the best decision, all of that information has to be researched to reduce uncertainty when trying to make the best choice. An overwhelming number of options could cause you to make a random choice, which may be a terrible choice. Or you may give-up and make no choice at all.

The wine expert may be able to provide advice on the different wines, their sweetness, the foods they complement, and the best vintages, to help you make the best choice. To get a similar comparison, you would need to try hundreds of wines using a trial-and-error approach over many years to find the one's you like most.

Another way to improve your judgment on a subject, is to become an expert yourself. Abraham Maslow once said that "sufficient knowledge" enables people to solve problems and helps them in their moral and ethical choices when deciding their next course of action. As people become more knowledgeable, their choices and solutions become easier and more automatic. Knowledge, he said, "brings certainty of decision, action, choice and what to do." Even in opening the abdomen, the surgeon knows to remove the inflamed appendix before it bursts and kills the patient. This, he says, is "an example of truth dictating what must be done."[38]

The result of having sufficient knowledge, or sufficient problem-solving skills, is that you are able to proceed confidently because you know what to do, or are able to figure out your next course of action. The purpose of programs designed to develop expertise is to provide the professional with the tools and techniques to reduce uncertainty when making costly decisions.

For example, a structural engineer may draw from one's training and expertise to identify structural deficiencies the average person would overlook. Finance experts have many mathematical models for calculating the risks associated with investment choices to reduce uncertainty, and the risk of financial losses, associated with investment decisions. Learning either of these the hard way could turn out to be a very expensive proposition that is far more likely to fail than it would succeed.

6

Suspending Judgment

People are naturally impulsive and impetuous, and pass judgment without fact-checking their conclusions. Suspending judgment is an exercise in self-restraint, to avoid passing judgment before you have enough information to be certain about a conclusion. This allows you to seek more complete and accurate information about a subject, to fill-in missing details and reduce errors when predicting the consequences of decisions. This is the "getting the facts necessary to know what you are talking about" part of using good judgment.

The ability to suspend your judgment is an exercise in recognizing whether you know enough to make an informed decision. This requires you to be honest about your knowledge, shortcomings, and cognitive limitations. Some people don't want to do that because of social pressures to appear self-confident, knowledgeable, and capable. This causes people to have, what some researchers call a Choice-Supportive Bias, where they believe their choices are more informed than they really are.

When you initially begin to collect information about a

choice, even a small detail could dramatically change your choice from one extreme to another. For example, suppose Margaret is moving to a new city. She's considering whether to move to the Towering Oaks neighborhood or the Winding Trails neighborhood. She really wants to live in a safe neighborhood that is close to work and her child's school. And the housing in Towering Oaks is affordable and meets her requirements. But after doing some research and talking to a real-estate agent, she discovers that Towering Oaks has one of the highest crime rates in the city and that Winding Trails is one of the safest. So, despite not getting exactly what she wanted, her research helped her make a better, more satisfactory, decision.

Passing judgment on someone before you have enough information is an example of a prejudgment or prejudice. In some circumstances where a judgment could influence how people are treated, prejudice can cause unnecessary adversity. When dealing with people or circumstances you know little about, you don't have to immediately pass judgment. If you are patient, and suspend your judgment long enough until you have enough information to know for certain, you will make better a decision.

7

Error-Checking

Ideally, people should be able to think critically about their own judgment to reduce errors and mistakes when making highly consequential decisions. Problems happen when a person is convinced about the correctness of a conclusion, but is, in fact, wrong. And when that person fails to fact-check that conclusion, especially when it is in doubt, that person may continue to act on that conclusion in error and make harmful mistakes. So, developing the habit of error-checking or fact-checking conclusions, especially when they are in doubt, can help you to avoid mistakes. But it's a habit that has to be developed with practice and exercise.

Being confident in your conclusions and believing you are correct is not enough to arrive at accurate, error free, judgment. You have to do research, collect evidence, fact-check, and make certain you are correct. You have to answer questions, like: Is my conclusion correct; am I being fair to this person; and what are the consequences if I'm wrong? This inner voice or moral conscience would be comparable to the popular phrase "think before you speak," or "think before you act."

When people fail to error-check their conclusions when making a critical decision that could harm people, it's not only wrong, in terms of being factually wrong, it could be morally and ethically wrong as well. This is a fact of moral judgment that many people have difficulty understanding.

Doing the right thing is not always easy. Making decisions with greater certainty involves acquiring information, asking questions, doing research, and fact-checking, to discover errors in your thinking and improve the accuracy of your judgment. If you are incapable of doing this, you will not only have more errors in your thinking and make more mistakes, you will experience more negative consequences associated with your decisions. This would be analogous to playing Russian roulette in which you never know what decision will end in catastrophe.

8
Modeling Techniques

Anytime you have a project, let's say you have a home renovation project, you likely have some idea, or mental model, of your project. Maybe you have some idea of what it will look like, how much money you want to spend, the number of hours you want to put into it, and so on. But unless you are a home remodeling expert, then your mental representation of what you want is likely filled with errors, inaccuracies, and missing information, like materials, costs, and measurements.

Documenting, and writing down, your idea on paper, rather than keeping it in memory, allows you to add details, list supplies, research materials and costs, take measurements, and create visual diagrams. This documentation helps you to quantify the project's size, cost, and time, to discover mistakes on paper beforehand and reduce uncertainty in your project. This is much less expensive than building a project that has serious problems, and then spending time and money to correct those mistakes after the fact.

Documentation, either on paper or by using software, also helps with team collaboration. This could be accomplished with visual illustrations, data models, visual diagrams, blue prints, whiteboarding, and charts. Suppose a project manager of a software engineering team has a new project. The client requesting the software knows what he wants, but is very short on details. He only provides a very brief and vague description of the proposed solution. To take on these difficulties, the project manager makes drawings, wireframes, mockups, and user stories, to illustrate how the software will be used. He, then, tests his models by showing his client the plans, and makes necessary corrections to the plans long before a significant amount of budgeted time, money, and resources are spent developing the solution. This is an example of how a project manager effectively reduces uncertainty about project requirements and guarantees the success of the project.

In the following sections, we look at a few examples of modeling techniques that make difficult, risky, or impactful, decisions more predictable, which prevents unnecessary losses, and improves the chances of success. Industry professionals typically use more advanced modeling techniques, requiring more math and skill than what is mentioned here. But the following examples have general application and could be used by anyone in their daily lives.

9

Scenario Analysis

You don't need a crystal ball to make predictions about consequences. In most daily circumstances, you only need to make a judgment about potential negative consequences and put measures in place to prevent those consequences. And a useful modeling technique for doing this is *scenario analysis*, in which you model different scenarios and make predictions about their consequences.

For example, suppose Sara is a Director of Information Technology at a large corporation. If Sara understands how her technology systems work, then she is already aware of why problems arise, like system failures, cyberbreaches, design mistakes, a lack of systems monitoring, or hardware failures. Any of these scenarios create uncertainty about potential downtime, lost revenue, lost customers, and exposed personal or intellectual property. And these problems can often be prevented, or mitigated, by hiring experts, doing research, and testing scenarios, to eliminate much of the worry about negative consequences. The more Sara considers and prepares for these scenarios, the more she can mitigate damage if they occur.

Suppose one day, Sara's company is hit with a ransomware attack, in which all files are encrypted and the cyber-criminals are demanding a ransom to decrypt the files. If their files are backed-up to a tape-drive or off-site backup that stores multiple versions of files, and Sara tested their backups, they should be able to quickly and easily recover their data without having to pay money to criminals. That's because, maybe as a result of training or previous experience, Sara has considered and prepared for that scenario. But if those scenarios are never considered, and Sara did not take those threats seriously, the consequences could be catastrophic to the business.

Scenario analysis can also be useful in your personal and professional life. Thinking about possible scenarios in your relationships, employment, and financial situation, can help you to prepare for, and take action, when potential problems arise. Everyone hopes they will never be the victim of a crime, or that they will never lose their job. But if you are prepared for those scenarios, you can more effectively mitigate potential losses. If you are remodeling your living space, you could easily predict the problems that could arise, beforehand, by imagining scenarios that would cause your project to fail, or cause set-backs, budget overruns, or predictable accidents. And that can help you avoid problems and determine the project's viability, even before you start.

10
Cost-Benefit Analysis

Ideally, your evaluation of your options and their consequences should be as objective as possible, for example, by reducing your options down to facts and numbers. And you can do that by doing cost-benefit analysis, which can help you calculate risks when making costly choices.

In corporate management, cost-benefit analysis uses data modelling and formulas to evaluate the costs and benefits of business decisions to maximize gains or minimize losses. But in your private life, cost-benefit analysis means weighing opportunity costs, or the opportunities you forego to obtain the things you want.

With every choice, you have an opportunity cost or a trade-off. You are forced to give up some things (e.g., time, money, or some other opportunity), to pursue what you want. For example, if you want to live a healthier lifestyle, then you need to give-up junk food and spend more time exercising. If you are a teenager, you may weigh the costs and benefits of playing video games with your friends during the weekend, or working at a local restaurant where you could save money and potentially land a higher paying job. All of these are opportunity costs where you end up forgoing some things to get what you want. And ultimately, you want to choose the options that yield the greatest payoff for you and your life goals.

Risk mitigation is an attempt to reduce the severity of losses, which is not the same thing as risk avoidance or risk aversion. It's not uncommon for a person to be risk averse because of inexperience that could lead to failure. But risk is in everything you do. As you strive to obtain the things you want in life you face uncertainty and risk losses or failure.

You could fail in your job, or be rejected in your relationships. In every business transaction, the buyer or seller risks losing money. So, you have to tolerate some risk, and expose yourself to the possibility of loss or failure or you will never achieve your goals. But you also want to mitigate those risks to avoid losing everything.

One way to mitigate risk is to avoid unnecessary risks. If you expose yourself to too much risk, you may face unnecessary and devastating consequences. Workers who drive themselves to work every day, risk getting into an accident. That is a normal risk. But some drivers drive too close to other vehicles, increasing their likelihood of getting into a serious accident. If an unexpected obstruction ends up in the lane, those drivers are not providing themselves or other drivers with enough time to stop, which guarantees a potentially life-threatening accident. That would be an example of an avoidable, and unnecessary, risk.

Big risks do not necessarily equate to big rewards. Quitting your job and getting a loan to finance a restaurant is certainly a big risk and could lead to big rewards. But if you lack a clear vision, a solid business plan, or a viable product, then you are exposing yourself to a high, and unmitigated, risk of losses and failure. Entrepreneurship, like all other life endeavors, involves risk. But you have to learn how use knowledge and skill to mitigate those risks and improve certainty in your success.

Another way to mitigate risk is by making decisions based on what you know for certain. If you want to build a restaurant, you need more than a belief that it will succeed. You need to create and test a menu, figure out where you are going to source your ingredients, calculate how much to charge, and figure out how much is required to cover your operating expenses. These are all things you can know beforehand, which can help mitigate risk. And you can use that knowledge to determine whether you have a viable business model, and how you need to improve your business model, before making the financial investment into your business.

Another way to mitigate risk is to create realistic and achievable goals, starting with realistic estimates for your time and budget. People are impatient and sometimes create unrealistic expectations for themselves or other people. If you put too much pressure on yourself to complete a time-consuming task in an unrealistic short period of time, you are likely to give-up and fail. Being patient and leveraging time by achieving smaller goals over a longer period of time, can give you a more solid footing to build on.

You could also slightly overestimate the amount of time and money required to finish a project, to prevent time and budget overruns. When making capacity planning decisions, planners sometimes budget for slightly more capacity than what is required to avoid falling short and making costly mistakes. Additionally, if your deadlines are short, you may put too much stress on yourself, which may cause you to make poor decisions or produce poor quality of work. If a work-related project takes three weeks to complete, plan to work on it for four weeks to allow for unforeseen events and challenges that will inevitably arise. This will help you to deliver on your promises, and produce satisfactory work, on a more consistent basis.

And lastly, you can mitigate risk by avoiding ventures that depend entirely on luck and chance, especially when the probability of achieving your desired goal is low. If a decision could result in one of two possible outcomes, then the probability of achieving your goal is the same as a coin flip, which is close 50 percent. As you increase the number of possible outcomes, assuming the result depends on chance, the probability of success in achieving the goal goes down, and the probability of failure goes up. Using methods that work with certainty and have a proven payoff can increase your odds of success.

11
Data Modeling & Artificial Intelligence

Computer technologies and artificial intelligence (AI) are increasingly providing ways to build better data models, to analyze costs and scenarios, and consider more factors that are beyond human intelligence. As computer scientists replicate human abilities using computer technologies, many of those technologies will be used as tools to inform human judgment so that people can make better decisions. And if AI designers want to make AI more autonomous and human like, with the ability to think independently and make decisions, they will also have to replicate the various abilities that makeup human judgment.

But to understand the advantages that AI provides, suppose a Scientist wanted to study the effects of human activity on Earth's climate. The researcher may need to calculate the population growth rate and the sales of polluting products to understand their impact on the environment. Knowing those consequences now, rather than in the future, would be better than living with the consequences in some dark, dystopian, future reality. But making those predictions is also highly complex because it involves many factors that Scientists may not understand or be aware of, which is where AI gains an advantage.

Increasingly, decision-makers are relying on data-models and computer simulations to test ideas, do scenario analysis, formulate strategies, establish goals, and make results-driven decisions. The more accurately data models represent the real-world, and contain real-world data, the more they can eliminate information-gaps that lead to wrong conclusions, and the more accurately they can predict real-world scenarios.

Founder and Chief Executive Officer of Bridgewater, Ray Dalio, recently published a book entitled *Principles: Life and Work*, about what made his billion-dollar investment firm successful.[10] According to Ray, part of what made his company successful was his careful observation of the factors influencing market conditions. Mr. Dalio would observe cause-and-effect relationships between economic influences, like rain fall, crop yields, and the price of feed for livestock. Or he would observe the effect of federal policy, or how demand for specific products influenced demand for commodities and precious metals. He would, then, write computer programs based on these data models to input different factors and run possible scenarios.

Overtime, his data gradually yielded more accurate predictions about financial markets when making investment decisions. Ray called this an ongoing cycle of trying, failing, learning from failures, making improvements, and trying again. And, despite not always being accurate, the market and investment models Ray created during his decades at Bridgewater helped to inform his judgment when making predictions about the market.

Computer technologies and artificial intelligence present many opportunities and risks. First of all, computer technologies have many advantages and capabilities over their human counterparts. They can observe more data types, store immense quantities of data, analyze and recognize complex patterns in immense datasets, and analyze complex and interrelated conditions. AI systems are potentially able to see patterns and identify risk factors in crime, poverty, or other social problems, that would be impossible to see, or act on, without those systems.

AI is capable of observing conditions the human brain is incapable of perceiving, and can consider factors that would, otherwise, be incomprehensible. This enables it to fill-in information gaps that are beyond human capabilities. It can observe phenomena that is instantaneously quick, or so slow it takes millions of years to observe, or is immensely huge, or infinitesimally small and requires microscopic technology. It can observe ultra-violet and infra-red spectrums that are too bright or too dim for human perception. And it can measure imperceptible forms of radiation. So, it's capable of creating data models that are more realistic, and information complete, and can enable decision-makers to make better decisions and solve, what would otherwise be, unsolvable problems.

Robots that connect to AI systems can automate tasks that people don't want to perform, or are incapable of performing. They can remain in the depths of space, or monitor vast regions of ocean, indefinitely, so long as they have a power source. They can perform dumb tasks much quicker, and without interruption, which would be too time-consuming, too complex, or too risky for people.

AI, and other new emerging technologies, may enable people to create things that would, otherwise, be impossible. It can enable doctors to rapidly diagnose conditions, edit genes, identify and treat diseases quicker, and create better solutions for disabilities. 3D design and printing technologies can enable designers to create more accurate scale models, build better prototypes, more sophisticated molds, and stronger, more durable, materials that are not possible using conventional production methods. These technologies could be used to design and create fantastic buildings and landscapes that are beyond human imagination.

12
Reality Testing

To know whether something works or not, you need to see it in action, whether it's an invention you constructed on paper, or a scientific hypothesis. And that is exactly what a reality test does. A *reality test* is a test of your ideas, or mental models, to see how well they work in reality.

For example, if you have a scientific hypothesis, which is nothing more than an unproven mental model of how reality works, then you could reality test that hypothesis to see if the model is correct. In another example, you could create a prototype, or a scaled-down example, of an invention you created on paper to test the viability of that idea. Doing this reveals details, and allows you to discover unexpected problems or unforeseen opportunities, that you could not consider otherwise.

This could also be called a "results-driven" approach. This should not be confused with the Machiavellian "ends justify the means" approach, and going to any lengths, including committing crimes or unethical behavior, to bring about a result. A *results-driven approach* relies exclusively on objective and measurable results to guide your decisions, rather than subjective hopes and wishes. In other words, you have to test your idea and see the results to understand where you need to improve and whether your effort is likely to succeed.

A results-driven approach tests and measures the ability to do something, rather than simply believing you can do it. The results of those tests will enable you to make a better judgment about how you are performing, and where you need to improve, rather than simply believing you will perform well. Basing your decisions on objective results (i.e., actual tests and measurements), rather than beliefs or guesses, will enable you to more accurately judge the consequences of that decision.

Some ideas are more difficult to test than others. Ideas that are validated mathematically, by quantifying time, physical dimensions, or costs, are typically easier to validate than those that involve human emotion or opinion. The quality of a stage performance, for example, depends on the opinions of the audience. Jim, who is an aspiring comedian, cannot really consider himself funny if no one else laughs at his jokes. If Jim wants to be a funny comedian, he has to test his performance to make certain his jokes are producing the intended result.

13

Critical Skills

When making critical and impactful decisions, people often make mistakes because of knowledge-gaps and missing information. So, you need to recognize when you have knowledge-gaps that could cause your judgment to be wrong. This may sound easy and straight forward. But it sometimes requires more work than it seems.

To make the best decision, you need to consider all of your options and opportunities. If you are not, then you are forcing yourself to make a less-than-desirable choice. You may also have an overwhelming number of options, which could cause you to make a random and undesirable selection. But you can make the selection process easier and more intuitive by doing research, or consulting with an expert, to narrow down your choice to a few easy and intuitive options.

The quality of your judgment depends on the quality of information upon which that judgment is based. So, you want information sources that are accurate and complete. One way of making certain your judgment is based on quality information is by separating subjective experience (i.e., low quality of information that tends to be incomplete and inaccurate) from objective results, or what is known and proven about objective reality. You need to recognize instances when you are basing your decisions on beliefs and believability, bad logic, and guesses, rather than relying more on credible sources of information, like science, expertise, proven facts, or objective measurements.

Gossip is another source of information that is highly subjective, and may not be the most credible source of information. You may have friends and family members whom you consider to be intelligent and credible. But unless they are experts on the subject in question, they may have poor memory, use bad logic, have ulterior motives, and make mistakes, even they are not aware of. And you don't have to offend them by pointing that out. Suspending your judgment until you have enough information, and error-checking your conclusions, are ways of reducing mistakes.

Another way of reducing uncertainty in decision-making, especially if you are working on a project, is to model your ideas on paper or by using software. If you can get the idea out of your head and on paper, it's easier to analyze and improve, and it can be shared with other team members.

Scenario analysis can help you analyze instances in which your idea could fail. It can help identify and prevent undesirable consequences, and plan a response in the event those consequences occur. And evaluate your choices by doing cost-benefit analysis. It can not only help you manage your time more wisely; it can help you prioritize the things you value the most.

And lastly, reality test your ideas to understand practical limitations and generate measurable results. If you can create a prototype, or scaled-down functioning model, of your idea, you can identify shortcomings and weaknesses that could cause your project to fail. And you can continue to work out the details until you are truly confident that your idea could work.

All of these techniques can help you avoid the perils of missing information and knowledge-gaps. But many other problems stem from poor judgment, like the ability to correctly attribute responsibility. Being able to do that can enable you to take more control over your own life and destiny. And that's exactly what we look at in the next part of this book.

PART II:
ASSESSING RESPONSIBILITY

Human judgment has a profound influence on how responsibly people behave, and whether they are able to correctly attribute responsibility. People are often not as responsible as they believe. And in the next chapter on personal responsibility, we look at some reasons people often struggle, and fail, to correctly assign blame. And in Chapter 4: Social Responsibility we look at the repercussions of decisions on people's lives, and how well intentions align with consequences.

CHAPTER 3:
PERSONAL RESPONSIBILITY

The idea of taking more responsibility may seem like a moot topic because it reminds us of what we need to do, what we are supposed to be doing, or what we have failed to do in striving to achieve our goals. The idea of taking more responsibility, can be a tall order. Maybe you are in a constant battle to keep-up with a demanding schedule as you pursue ambitious goals. Or, you are constantly responding to the demands of family members, coworkers, or managers. It always seems like we could do a little more, work a little harder, or be a little more prepared, to succeed in achieving our goals. So, the idea of taking more responsibility, can be overwhelming, exhausting, and stressful to many people.

But the idea of taking more responsibility is desirable because it means gaining greater control and choice over the direction of your life, so you are not at the mercy of circumstance. And you would want other people to be more responsible as well because it reduces social problems that have a negative impact on people's lives and the community. And since adults are considered to be legally responsible for their decisions, it makes sense that they also know what it means to accept that responsibility.

In this chapter, we also look at the ability to correctly attribute responsibility. When people are unable to do that, it's often called an attribution error, or an error in judgment where blame is wrongly assigned. These errors are sometimes intentional, for example, when a person wants to avoid blame, or put the blame on others, for terrible a decision. But it also happens when a person is in an unfortunate situation and is blamed for creating the problems one is experiencing. Later, in this chapter, we look at these types of attribution errors and some common reasons they occur.

1

Defining Responsibility

If you researched the dictionary definition of responsibility, you would find a variety of definitions that include: Having a duty or obligation to fulfill; being accountable; having the ability to act independently; or being a source of blame. Responsibility, in this book, is generally defined as a person's ability to accept blame for a decision and its consequences.

Responsibility comes in a variety of forms as it applies to different life roles, like parenting, management, or being a responsible citizen. Under the law, you have legal responsibility. For example, in many local jurisdictions in the United States, if your pet injures someone and you do not restrain your pet or provide warning, you may be held legally responsible for their injuries. Irresponsible behavior, on the other hand, usually involves instances in which people behave recklessly and carelessly and may try to avoid blame for their behavior. Some examples include crime or corruption, in which a person is hurting other people for one's own personal or financial gain and wants to avoid any negative consequences.

2
Learning Responsibility

Learning to be responsible requires more than memorizing a "canned" dictionary definition of the word responsibility. You need to understand the repercussions, and higher-order consequences, of decisions, how to improve your judgment when assigning blame, and how your decisions impact people's lives. The problem is, people are not always as responsible as they believe. Even those who are highly successful, who are thought of as highly responsible because of their business success, can sometimes make mistakes for which they do not want to accept responsibility. Learning how to correctly attribute responsibility is a skill that can improve with practice and life experience.

Parents sometimes try to teach responsibility by setting expectations for their children. For example, by following rules, doing chores, making good grades in school, taking care of their possessions, and looking after their siblings. Those chores give children a greater sense of obligation to fulfill their responsibilities. But simply doing what you are told is a very minimal form of responsibility. It does not put into perspective other types of responsibility, like skills development, or actions that impact the lives of others.

Personal responsibility is also not entirely a generalized skill, meaning that simply because you have developed thinking and behavioral habits that have made you responsible in performing one task, does not mean that you are capable of being highly responsible in others. For example, a person may be highly responsible when it comes to one's career, but may be completely irresponsible when it comes to one's family. Or a business owner may excel in product development and sales, but is careless about how employees are treated, or how the business is negatively impacted by poor management or poor business practices.

3

Attributing Responsibility

Anytime a problem arises, and you use your judgment to determine who or what caused that problem, you are attributing responsibility to some cause. This is similar to how a police detective identifies who is responsible for a crime, or a medical doctor diagnosing the cause of an illness. When people use good judgment, and accurately attribute responsibility to the correct cause, it not only accelerates the resolution of problem, in many cases, it can create a sense of fairness and justice. The inability to do that, as we have already seen, is often called an attribution error.

Attribution errors can create serious problems when people automatically put blame on others for problems that were truly not their fault. And that can sometimes be very socially and financially condemning. People wrongly attribute responsibility, even to their own behavior. Consider, for example, a tennis player who is playing terribly and blames it on the tennis racket. Or consider Tim who is late to work and gets angry at a slow driver for cutting him off, when the driver really did nothing wrong. Tim is the one responsible for planning his morning commute and arriving to work on time.

Part of the problem with correctly attributing responsibility is understanding scope of responsibility, which encompasses what you have control over. To a limited extent, you have the ability to increase your scope of responsibility, for example, by doing more things for yourself, rather than expecting other people to do it for you. And later in this chapter, we look at some reasons why doing that can be advantageous. But people tend to have problems attributing responsibility when they believe they have more, or less, control over world affairs than they really do.

An example of this is when a person believes that one is responsible for causing events that one had no control over. A mother may feel guilty for her child's sickness and wonders what she did wrong to deserve it. Or a crime victim may say that he did not protect himself enough from the criminal who harmed him. The victim is not responsible for committing the crime and should not take responsibility for the consequences, even when he could have done more to protect himself.

On the other side of the problem, people sometimes believe they have less responsibility than they really do. For example, you are responsible for maintaining your vehicle even when you know nothing about vehicle maintenance. If your car dies because you never changed the motor oil, you could say: "I was not aware of that." While that statement may be true, it does not make you less responsible for your vehicle. In that instance, you would use better judgment to have it regularly checked by a reputable auto-mechanic.

Defining a realistic scope of responsibility is important for using good judgment. All people have limitations in cognitive ability and constraints in time, money, and other resources, and are capable of handling only a limited amount of responsibility. If you are a manager and assign a worker the workload of five people, that may create unrealistic expectations about that person's performance. Or maybe a stressed-out parent, who is juggling dozens of daily tasks, may accidentally forget to do something. That does not mean that those people are irresponsible. In fact, it may mean they are trying to juggle too many responsibilities.

4
Product of Circumstance

Overestimating your responsibility in world affairs can cause errors in judgment. In reality, you are not responsible for everything that happens to you. Your life, in many ways, is a product of circumstance that is shaped by fortunate opportunities and unfortunate events. Psychologist Julian Rotter called this idea that life is, partly, shaped by forces beyond your control, your *external locus of control*.

All people live with some sense of powerlessness as their lives are shaped by forces beyond their control. Not only are you unable to control the forces of nature, in many ways, you have no control over your own biology and cognitive limitations, making it impossible to foresee the consequences of every decision. You do not have a choice about your genes, or the political or economic conditions in which you grew up. And you cannot control past events, what people think, or the help you receive.

In many circumstances, people are incapable of being fully responsible for their lives. Children who are not fully developed need a caregiver to provide, and make, choices for them. People who have age-related conditions, like Alzheimer's disease, or certain types of disabilities or disorders, may have problems forgetting or attending to responsibilities.

Even your personality partially develops in response to environmental demands. My experience from living in different cities has shown me that people who live in poorer, higher crime-rate, communities tend to be more protective, defensive, and less trusting toward strangers, than people who live in wealthier, lower crime-rate, communities. Different conditions provide different opportunities, present different challenges, and elicit different responses that promote different personality traits.

The truth is, the world can be hard on people for no fault of their own. And it's important to understand this fact when judging people without understanding their struggles, difficulties, and adverse life experiences.

5

Product of Choice

You may not have absolute control over many things in your life, but you do mostly have control over your choices. You can choose how you develop, how much time you spend being productive and developing skills, how much you help the people around you, and how you perform different life roles. And you may not choose the problems you face, but you do choose how you resolve them. Psychologist Julian Rotter called this idea that your life is, partly, shaped by your own choices, your *internal locus of control*.

The choices you make overtime has a cumulative influence on your life successes. For example, a sports reporter may focus on the player's decisions during the final seconds of the game that caused the team to win or lose. But many factors actually contributed to the team's victory or defeat, like practice, diet, exercise, and strategy. Games are sometimes won or lost long before the players step onto the field. And improving performance with physical conditioning, testing abilities and scenarios, comparing the numbers, and having determination and persistence, all influence the final result.

Most adults are also responsible for making healthy lifestyle choices. In modern economies, like the United States, consumers are surrounded by advertisements enticing them to consume unhealthy food and beverages. Even when you give-in to those ads, those companies are not responsible for your unhealthy diet. In fact, you can find many people who live in that same market environment who make very healthy lifestyle choices. Education, and the availability of healthy food, can also make a difference. For example, if you don't know how to make a healthy and delicious meal, then you are more likely to make an unhealthy choice. So, some of that responsibility may involve learning and skills development.

6

Answering for Decisions

Public judgment, and the need for personal acceptance, inevitably forces people to answer for their decisions. The problem is, as people strive to keep up with a demanding schedule, earn a living, and take care of their family, they will inevitably make mistakes and have shortcomings in their abilities. The question is: How do you answer for those mistakes or shortcomings?

Ideally, people would be honest and accept responsibility, not only for the life achievements they take pride in, but for their mistakes and shortcomings as well. When people identify, and take responsibility for, problems, it provides them with objective feedback about their performance so they can make changes to prevent those problems from occurring in the future. When a person refuses to accept blame for a poor decision, that person is not learning from that mistake, making it more likely that person will repeat that mistake in the future.

Unfortunately, not everyone thinks this way. Some people view any accusation of a mistake, or any form of blame, as an attack on their character. After all, they could get fired from their employment, especially if a law was broken. So, to prevent those character attacks, sometimes people lie, deny responsibility, or put the blame on someone else, as a way to avoid condemning judgment and adverse treatment. This is similar to a defendant in criminal trial lying to deny responsibility for a crime to avoid punishment. People want to avoid negative consequences, even for the acts they commit. So, they will sometimes deny, or avoid, responsibility, not because they are diabolical and wicked, but because they want to protect themselves from negative consequences, and from a less positive version of reality than the one they are experiencing.

Answering for decisions can force people to recognize and acknowledge their own bad behavior. But people who are in positions of power are often not required to answer for their decisions. People answer to them, not the other way around. So, some people in positions power sometimes lack the obligation to recognize their own bad behavior. And that can be very corrupting when it allows a person to say or do anything, for any reason, and hurt or take advantage of others, without ever having to face consequences.

7

Character Defenses

Anytime someone is threatened by condemning accusations that would result in rejection, adverse treatment, or losses in the form of friends, employment, or finances, it can trigger an effort to fight-off that threat, which we call a defense mechanism, or character defense. *Character defenses* are an attempt to protect your interests and influence outcomes by defending your actions from accusations of negligence or wrongdoing. In other words, your character defenses kick-in whenever you stand to gain or lose something.

Character defenses can manifest in a variety of forms. On an instinctive level, the display of anger is an emotional defense, the outward characteristics of which provides physical and emotional protection. Physiologist Walter Cannon once described the defense of anger as expressing itself in the bristling of hair and uncovering of teeth in rage and hostility. The "rage response," as he called it, is displayed in a "crouching body," a "frowning brow," and "grinding teeth." The individual mutters "growled threats," has "tightened fists," and seizes a weapon in preparation for attack. All of these behaviors, he says, are useful in preparation for the struggle.[5]

People are usually not that overly dramatic when they get angry. But fear, and the desire for protection, compels people to thoughtlessly pulverize any pestilent little thing that threatens their interests, no matter how small or insignificant it is. This desire for protection is territorial, in a way. People see value in protecting things that could be taken from them, like employment, an intimate relationship, or a material possession, which can provoke a response to defend it, or take it back. A child may express this most uninhibitedly when a toy or food is taken away, especially when the child begins to cry, kick, or scream, because someone threatens to deprive him of the thing he wants. But adults can behave similarly when they throw fits, lie, or start arguments, to get what they want.

Your natural defenses are continuously working to protect you from various threats to your physical wellbeing, as well as threats to your social and financial status. And people are naturally compelled to defend their actions, especially when those actions are believed to be based on sound reasoning. To that end, people will sometimes lie to justify their actions, to protect themselves from accusations of wrongdoing, or to promote themselves as being better than they really are.

In the next few sections, we look at a few different types of character defenses including blaming, rationalization, deception, and obstruction. Many of these defenses are perfectly legitimate, like when someone else is responsible for a failure, or that failure was caused by factors beyond your control. But people can also behave carelessly and recklessly, and may not want to accept blame, or suffer the consequences, for a preventable failure. Learning how to spot these types of character defenses can help you to avoid attribution errors.

8

Blaming

When a person does not want to accept responsibility, or blame, for a decision, a natural tendency is to attribute responsibility, or blame, other people or circumstances. It is possible that other people, or circumstances, are legitimately to blame for causing a problem. Suppose a worker, who has a very good attendance record, is late one day and blames it on road construction. That may be a perfectly legitimate defense, since the worker was not able to predict the construction and did not have a choice in the matter. But if a person is late every day for months, and blames it on slow traffic, that may not be a legitimate defense since the person can easily predict and prepare for slow traffic and has a choice of whether to leave earlier.

A *scapegoat* is someone, or something, that people blame for misfortune. Abusers tend to scapegoat, and put blame on, their victims for example. And one way they succeed in doing that is by isolating the victim so the abuse is not revealed, or to make it look like the victim deserves the treatment by saying horrible things to bias people's opinions about the victim. Scapegoating also happens in business, when managers put blame on subordinates or third-party contractors to scapegoat them for any problems that may arise in a project.

Alfred Adler once gave example of a person who wanted to deny ever making mistakes and, instead, wanted to blame his parents or education. He complained that nobody ever cared for him and that he was mistreated. He wanted to be "excused of further responsibility" to avoid all criticism and blame. The reason he could never fulfill his life ambitions was always someone else's fault. He never changed his behavior, but "turns and twists and distorts his experiences until they fit it." Even the child, Adler said, creates excuses for his failures, claiming that he was "too weak or petted," or siblings thwarted his development.[1]

The fact that our personal development is, to some extent, shaped and nurtured by other people, like caregivers, educators, trainers, and managers, makes it easy to pass blame onto them for our shortcomings. And despite the fact that, as an adult, you are responsible for your own personal development, some people take rationalization to its furthest extent and blame all of their problems on anything that is larger or more powerful than themselves.

In *Totem and Taboo* published in 1913, Sigmund Freud

called this tendency a "delusion of persecution," in which a person's power over life-circumstances is so immensely exaggerated that every disagreeable experience falls under the responsibility of the more powerful person. He pointed out that savages blamed their kings because they had enormous power and, therefore, power over the forces of nature. This, he said, arose from the heavy burden of being dependent on someone who is more powerful, where it puts the individual in a position of blame for all misfortunes.[18]

Blame can go in the other direction as well, when leaders blame subordinates for problems that arise under their leadership. Ideally, managers would take responsibility for the trajectory of the business by reviewing the quality of their work, and ensuring that workers have the resources and training to perform the work. Instead, you will find managers who put the blame on workers, technological complexity, shortages in the labor market, or circumstances beyond their control. And that denial of responsibility only leaves the underlying problems in the organization unresolved.

9

Rationalization

People want to believe, and want others to believe, that their behavior is rational and that their actions are justified. *Rationalization* is an attempt to explain, or prove, that one's actions are justified, usually to avoid negative judgment and potential adverse treatment. Eric Fromm once gave an example of how the "function of rationalization," enables a person to "prove to himself and to others that his action is determined by reason, common sense, or at least conventional morality." And no matter how "unreasonable or immoral an action may be, man has an insuperable urge to rationalize it."[19]

The idea of rationalization as a character defense comes from the idea that people usually do not want to think of themselves as evil, diabolical, villains, no matter how malicious or hateful they are. Instead, it's more desirable to see oneself as a rational person whose actions are fully justified. When a person acts out on emotion, or engages in careless or reckless behavior that causes harm or damage, one way to escape the consequences may be to lie to create reasons for those actions.

Even when people have good intentions, those people may ultimately be judged by the consequences of their actions. Intentions do matter. But people have to live with, and maybe suffer from, real-world consequences. This is why exercising good judgment, practicing due-diligence, and mitigating risks are so important. Even a person with good intentions can do serious damage if that person is unable to question and think critically about one's actions.

10

Deception

People are not always incentivized to be honest, especially when their decisions could result in negative consequences. Some people lie about their achievements or skills to obtain a better paying employment position. Criminals use these tactics to avoid being arrested by law enforcement or to avoid going to prison in criminal trials. But you can also see it when a person makes a poor decision, or behaves badly, and wants to avoid condemning judgment or rejection.

Deception, and the ability to lie and manipulate facts in one's favor, is learned at a very early age as we can observe in children, when a child throws screaming fit because of an unfulfilled want, or acts differently around people who provide attention or money. When adults exhibit these behaviors, they are sometimes called narcissists or two-faced liars.

Often times, dishonesty and deception are not crimes and are not used for malicious reasons. For example, political campaigns may try to influence voter choices by leading them to believe things that are untrue about the other candidate. Or a sign in front of a restaurant may say that it is the #1 Hot Dog Restaurant in Town for 30 years, despite the fact that it is consistently rated as the worst restaurant in town. Businesses exaggerate the greatness of their products to attract customers. Similarly, elected officials exaggerate their accomplishments to win voters.

In the words of Niccolo Machiavelli in his book *the Prince*, "men judge by the eye rather than the hand, for all men can see a thing, but few come close enough to touch it. All men will see what you seem to be; only a few will know what you are, and those few will not dare to oppose the many who have the majesty of the state on their side to defend them. In all men's acts"..."it is the result that renders the verdict when there is no court of appeal."[36]

Deception exploits a weakness in judgment whereby, in the absence of knowledge, people tend to believe things that are believable and disbelieve things that are unbelievable. That weakness is what enables con-artists to paint a believable picture of reality to influence the outcome in their favor. In the criminal world, the con-artist exploits this weakness in judgment for the purpose committing crimes, like illicitly obtaining money or property. The con-artist lies by assuming a false identity to gain unauthorized access to information or possessions, or manipulates perceptions to avoid being caught. Or an abuser may frame a victim as someone who is crazy, genetically defective, mentally un-stable, or as someone who cannot be believed or trusted. All of these play into people's beliefs and biases, which are nothing more than weaknesses in their judgment.

11

Obstruction

People sometimes try to coverup and hide behavior or char-acter flaws they do not want others to know about, that could subject them to accusations of wrongdoing or guilt. Using obstruction, people attempt to influence outcomes by preventing others from seeing the truth, hiding anything that would be incriminating, or would attribute wrongdo-ing.

Obstruction can be learned during childhood. The child wants to please the caregiver who provides food, play-things, and safety. So, when something is accidentally bro-ken, the child learns to hide it and act innocent to prevent the caregiver's anger and scorn. Even as a child grows into adulthood, young people learn that they can get ahead by hiding weaknesses, insecurity, or guilt, by using deception to avoid admitting shortcomings. This follows the tendency that people want to accept responsibility for the positive things they do, not the terrible things that subject them to condemning judgment or punishment.

Obstruction can also be used to hide behavioral patterns that are generally not socially acceptable, like substance abuse or domestic violence. Those patterns sometimes emerge in the presence of different people in different envi-ronments. A person, who is a monster to a family member, may be the kindest and most caring person to managers and coworkers. It all depends on the nature of their relationship, and what they stand to gain or lose from the relationship.

Repression is way of obstructing oneself from one's own problems. And sometimes, repression can be beneficial when it allows a person to overcome unnecessary guilt and move on with life, instead of being discouraged by failures, mistakes, inadequacies, or carnal desires. But repression can also do unnecessary harm and work against the welfare of people, when a person ignores physical pain that turns out to be a cancerous tumor, or when a person ignores a loud bang that turns out to be a murder. People will also repress guilt for the crimes they have committed to live more confidently within themselves.

12
Taking Responsibility

Ideally, you want to increase your scope of responsibility, so you can take more control over your fate and influence outcomes, rather than allowing other people or circumstances to control your destiny. This is an act of taking more responsibility. For example, you can take more control over your own development by further developing your skills. By taking the initiative, you stand a better chance at making things happen, rather than allowing things to happen to you and being dissatisfied with the result. If you simply wait for that lucky moment when fortune changes your life, then you will always have bad luck, and unfortunate circumstances, to blame for your lack of success.

The first step in taking more responsibility is by focusing on your internal locus of control and recognizing your role in creating your situation, rather than focusing on how misfortune and forces beyond your control created your situation. By identifying your shortcomings and failures, and the choices that contributed to your current situation, you can begin to establish goals, and make choices, that will help you overcome those shortcomings, like pursuing the skills you want to develop. The only downside is that you have to do more work and put more effort to make things happen in your life.

To illustrate this, imagine you purchase take-out food from a local restaurant. You get home and notice an item is wrong and a family member is upset and will not eat the food. At first, you blame the worker who put the order together, and for good reason. But you also had responsibility to make sure the order was correct before leaving. You could have discovered and corrected the mistake and left with the order you paid for. Even when other people do not behave responsibly, you are still responsible for creating the outcomes you want. And you will not be satisfied with your life if you allow other people to make too many decisions for you. Those people will always be to blame for the problems you experience.

Another way to take more responsibility for your life is seeking objective feedback about shortcomings in your performance. The problem with making a critical assessment about your own performance is that it becomes a matter of subjective opinion, which is heavily influenced by biases and character defenses. But you can also measure your performance by pursuing academic courses or taking tests, which can provide you with feedback on where to improve. Reality has no substitutes. So, the more objective you can make your assessments, the closer to reality the achievement of your goal will become.

My own strategy in taking more responsibility when stepping into a new role is to become a problem solver, or a person who prioritizes and resolves preventable problems that lead to dissatisfaction. This means scanning the environment and identifying problems that could lead to negative consequences. Doing that allows me to create a list of to-dos and goals to work toward. The quicker these problems can be prioritized and resolved, the fewer problems and greater satisfaction can be experienced in the future.

13

Giving Responsibility

You cannot be everywhere and know everything. And sometimes its advantageous to give responsibility to another person, or business, for completing a task. And you can be far more effective, and more productive, if you leverage the help of others and delegate tasks to those who may perform those tasks better than you. But that also means putting trust in people and having confidence in their abilities.

Two common reasons people delegate tasks are time and expertise. Sharing responsibility and working as a team means getting more done in less time. You could do the work of ten people, but it would take you ten times as long, if not longer. Delegating tasks to other people allows you to accomplish more in less time at a higher quality of production, which frees you up to pursue other goals.

Another reason you may delegate responsibility is for tasks you are not particularly good at, or don't know how to perform, because they are beyond your skillset. You cannot be an expert in everything. And usually, people in developed economies pay people or businesses to do things for them, like prepare their meals or make their possessions. This allows them to get back to doing what they do best. For example, you may be able to fix a home appliance after you have watched enough online videos. But, unless you are an expert, your knowledge of appliance repair is not going to be as good as the expert who repairs appliances for a living. So, instead of spending hours trying to fix it, and not knowing if you have the tools, you may be better off delegating that task to a professional.

If you are delegating a task in which you have expertise, you may need to provide training and testing to make sure the task is being performed correctly. You should also monitor the quality of production to make sure they are delivering on their promises. And establish an agreement, like a verbal agreement or written contract. This establishes an expectation about the work to be performed, the quality of that work, and the deliverables to be expected. And it creates a reasonable basis for terminating the work if the agreement is broken.

15
Critical Skills

Correctly attributing responsibility can help you diagnose the root causes of the problems you face. Attribution errors occur for many reasons. A person may refuse to accept blame for a decision, or the consequences of that decision. Or, a person may accept credit for work they did not do. Or, a person may wrongfully attribute blame to others for problems they did not create. Rather than attributing responsibility based on limited information, like gossip, your beliefs, your emotions, or appearances, you may need to do more thinking and investigative work to correctly attribute responsibility.

When making critical decisions, consider how you will

answer for your decisions if you are questioned or con-fronted. People naturally want to avoid blame and con-demning judgment, and may try to lie to avoid responsibil-ity for mistakes. When people rely on dishonesty and de-ception, either to make themselves appear more accom-plished, or to avoid blame by covering up mistakes or short-comings, it becomes difficult to trust that person. People who are more honest and up-front about their actions are not only more trustworthy, they are more highly motivated to do a better job and avoid mistakes.

Take more responsibility for your successes or failures by being more involved in efforts. If you allow other people to do too much for you, and they make mistakes, you will never be satisfied and will always have other people to blame for your problems. Delegate responsibility for tasks you do not have time for, or that other people can do better. If you take on too much responsibility, it can increase your stress levels and cause you to make poorer decisions, reduce the amount of time available to you, and potentially reduce your quality of work. When delegating responsibility, set expectations in a verbal agreement or written contract to make certain those people are delivering on their promises.

CHAPTER 4:
SOCIAL RESPONSIBILITY

Social responsibility is the credit or blame attributed to you for the impact your decisions have on yourself, other people, or the environment. In other words, social responsibility focuses on consequences and using your judgment to assess the impact, or repercussions, of a decision on the lives of other people. Social responsibility is not only about reducing the negative impact decisions have on the world, but it can also be about making a positive impact, by contributing to community or charitable organizations.

The problem is, many people do not understand, or even care about, the full impact their decisions have on other people's lives, especially when their own lives are not being directly impacted. An obvious example of this would be someone dumping toxic chemicals into a river that people and wildlife use as a water source, and then assuming the problem will simply go away. Or in instances of crime or corruption, the perpetrator is making gains at the expense of others, like in an act of theft, robbery, or embezzlement.

You can find many examples of people make poor decisions without fully understanding, or caring about, the impact it has on other people's lives. That can happen because the individual is experiencing high levels of stress, or because of carelessness. For example, a police officer who, as a result of job-related stress, shoots and kills an innocent person believing that person was a crime suspect. Or a Human Resources person who makes up a lie to get an employee fired for filing a hostile workplace report. In both cases, the decision-maker is making wrong assumptions or using bad logic while making little, or no, conscious effort to minimize the impact one has on the lives of others. The first approach in each of these cases should be to minimize the negative impact toward those involved.

Another problem is when policy makers create policies that may be heavily influenced by their own personal biases without fully assessing the impact. An example of this would be assuming a bridge is safe without having a structural engineer look at it. Or a policy may apply across the board, when it should exclude the people or business's that could be negatively impacted by the policy.

1

Forms of Social Responsibility

Social responsibility comes in a variety of forms, from your social obligation as a citizen to corporate or governmental social responsibility. Your personal social responsibility includes those acts that have a positive or negative impact on people's lives or the community. For example, as a citizen, you can have a positive impact by helping a community organization or by simply obeying laws.

Usually, when the term social responsibility is used, it refers to corporate or governmental social responsibility. Corporate social responsibility focuses on the impact that a business has on communities or the environment, like the impact of defective products on consumers, the treatment of labor, or the pollution created as a result of doing business. Economists call these negative repercussions, negative externalities, or the cost of doing business that taxpayers agree to pay for. Government interventions can incentivize private individuals and businesses to be more environmentally responsible by imposing fines for actions that pollute the environment.

Political social responsibility tends to focus on the impact that laws and public programs have on a community and, therefore, is often a very divisive issue that is subject to many opinions and interpretations. And in this chapter, we briefly look at some examples of failed policies, or policies that have easily predictable and preventable negative repercussions. My readers should not consider these views as politically motivated, but instead as practical examples of what can go wrong.

2

Responsible Use of Power

Social power is the ability to control another person's behavior. And behavior can be controlled by means of influence, persuasion, organizational position, money, threats, and coercion. Money, by itself, gives you some limited power as a citizen, but not necessarily the power hurt, or take advantage of, people against their will. Those acts are typically considered to be forms of corruption.

Corruption has many definitions and comes in many forms. But in this book, corruption refers to people who misuse their powers and privileges, usually to hurt, or take advantage of, people. Forms of corruption are found in every organization. And many are harmless and negligible, like mismanagement, abuses of privileges, or violating company policies. Other forms of corruption can devastate lives and businesses.

Power and money, alone, are not necessarily corrupting. Or as the popular phrase goes: "power tends to corrupt, and absolute power corrupts absolutely," written by John Dalberg-Acton in a letter to an Anglican bishop.[31] But power provides you with the ability to further your own interests, which gives you the ability to do more of what you want. Power reveals what a person would do with power if one had it. Some people seem like the most scrupulous and honest people. But the moment you give them power, suddenly they wanted to use that power to hurt, or take advantage of, people. The problem is not with power or money, by itself. The problem is with what people intend to do with that power.

The causes of corruption can be divided into several categories, including matters of accountability, matters of competency and skill, and matters of prejudice and ingroup biases. The first of these, which I will call matters of accountability, occurs when certain people within an organization are exempt from accountability. In other words, even when they violate policies or commit crimes, they never have to face consequences, which would allow those problems to continue or grow worse overtime. And that is especially true for business owners who have sole authority over the organization and cannot be reprimanded or fired for bad behavior.

People in positions of authority have the power to hire and fire people, restructure the organization, write the rules that govern operations, and even systematically exempt themselves or other people from having to answer for their decisions. Obedience to authority is imperative to the success of many organizations, for example, the Military. One of the reasons obedience to authority is a core value of the Military in nations around the world, is that failing to follow the orders and execute a strategy as it was designed, could result in horrible consequences, preventable deaths, or failing relations between nations that result in more conflict.

Reporting is one of the best ways to bring about better accountability. The only problem is, some managers view reports as micromanaging or not trusting the authority of their managers. So, when a worker files a report of abuse, management may view that worker as "unhappy" or "disgruntled" with how the business is managed and may decide that person would be better off discharged from that position. That, of course, does not resolve the underlying problem being reported. And if management simply makes-up a lie to terminate that worker's employment, that worker may be denied employment insurance because the employer is lying about the reason for termination. And despite what people believe about wrongful termination lawsuits, or whistle-blower lawsuits, that worker may have zero legal recourse to do anything about it in many United States jurisdictions.

Another cause of corruption involves incompetence or skills deficits. Just as people want to protect and maintain their interests, one of those interests is their employment and income. And one way of doing that is by, what some people call, earning their position by working hard, obeying the rules, and developing skills that improve their performance. But some people end up in positions for different reasons. A manager may put friends or relatives in positions for which they are unquailed and are incapable of performing.

Corruption, in this instance, has nothing to do with the inclusion of friends and family, who may be qualified and skilled for the position. Often friends and family help to get a business started, or a business may be a family operated business. But corruption, in this instance, occurs because the manager is knowingly putting an unqualified person in a position that requires qualifications.

When a person has skills deficits, shortcomings in knowledge, and frequently makes mistakes, that's often a motive to terminate that person's employment. And could, in turn, motivate dishonesty to coverup those deficits and mistakes, or to find a way to put the blame on other people. A person who lacks credentials may not be incentivized to see the value in credentials and may consider them unnecessary. That person may have difficulty taking responsibility for training subordinates, or monitoring the quality of production, both of which decrease the quality of the product.

Added to that is the fear that one could be replaced by a more qualified and knowledgeable candidate. A manager in that position would be less incentivized to congratulate others and give them credit for their work. Or worse, they may lie to get those people fired, to eliminate the threat all together. And management may be more inclined to believe friends and family they are obligated to, over the claims of strangers. The negative outcomes caused by skills deficits, only incentivizes dishonesty and other dramatic attempts to avoid employment termination. And that can create a vary unwelcoming and hostile environment for skilled and qualified professionals. When recruiters and hiring managers automatically assume employers are operating responsibly, they tend to automatically put the blame on workers after an employment termination, no matter the reason.

Corruption is also caused by prejudices and ingroup biases. Employees feel pressure to obediently adopt the opinions of organizational leaders, or their peers, as a way of preventing disagreement and conflict, and protecting their employment. So, if a manager makes a racists or sexist statement, a subordinate may chuckle uncomfortably and agree to avoid getting on the manager's bad side.

3

Systems of Accountability

Holding someone accountable for one's behavior is an act of attributing responsibility to a decision or its consequences. Just as an Accountant keeps a system of ledgers to record business decisions that involve revenues and expenditures, people are able to keep a mental ledger of their own contributions and those of other people. Any time a person is formally held responsible for a decision that resulted in a gain or loss, or a decision that had a positive or negative impact, that is a form of accountability.

Systems of accountability can reduce forms of crime and corruption by making sure that people are held accountable for decisions that impact other people's lives. In fact, modern societies have many different ways of holding people accountable for decisions that have a positive or negative impact on communities. The criminal justice system, for example, punishes people for actions that cause harm. The legal system provides services to victims to help them find justice for actions that resulted in unfair losses, and in some instances, to recover those losses. The news media in the United States is free to report on decisions made by public figures that positively or negative impact people's lives. Imagine if no one knew that a business was dumping toxic chemicals into a river that people and wildlife were using as a water source. The freedom of media to report on these topics is what motivates action to improve life for all people.

Within organizations, systems of accountability can also account for gains and losses made by decisions-makers. And in many instances, these systems can be highly objective and driven by facts and numbers. In fact, the more objective these systems of accountability are, the fairer they are to employees, which can improve employee satisfaction. For example, if you have a merit system, and you are putting highly skilled people in senior level positions, it can improve training and increase human capital.

It can incentivize good decisions by crediting those that result in wanted gains, or sanctioning those that result in unwanted losses. This may also require better reporting and policing of actions that cause harm, conflict, negligence, or preventable losses, so that management can take action to further prevent those losses. Without these systems, decision-makers within the organization would be allowed to repeatedly make terrible decisions that negatively impact the organization or the lives of people.

An example of this would be an *incentive system* that rewards, or compensates, workers based on the value they bring and takes corrective action for decisions that negatively impact the organization. Studies have shown that rewarding workers for positive contributions, acknowledges the value of their work, and leads to improved employee satisfaction and better retention. Providing rewards when workers deserve it, validates their contributions and encourages employees to repeat those behaviors.[53]

A *merit system* is another way to hold people accountable by promoting them based on credentials, expertise, and skills. Ideally, employers pay for skills since that's what brings value to the organization. Without skills and knowhow, management is forced to hire outside labor to perform that work, which can be an expensive and wasteful proposition. So, hiring and promoting workers based on the value they bring not only improves efficiencies and reduces costs, it puts people in positions who are most capable of creating the most value for the organization.

Incentive systems and merit systems do not always work effectively, especially when they are heavily influenced by biases. Ideally, management would hand out rewards for achieving specific, and perhaps difficult, goals. But some managers may arbitrarily hand out rewards for no good reason believing that it will improve performance. Or a manager may only favor select individuals, like friends, family members, or a favored team member, rather than thinking more objectively about the contributions of all the team members. When management hands out rewards based on objective measures, rather than personal prefer- ences, it creates a fairer workplace that should improve worker satisfaction and retention.

4

Responsible Policy

Laws and policies usually try to influence how people and businesses operate in a way that reduces negative repercus- sions on communities. If business and free enterprise were like a game, to use an analogy, then laws and regulations would be like the rules of the game designed to ensure some fairness among the players. For example, government may try to incentivize businesses to reduce pollution, which im- proves the quality of life for citizens in communities. But in- tuitively knowing the full impact of a law or policy can be difficult.

Policy decisions today are heavily influenced by intuition, financial or political interests, social biases and beliefs, and political affiliations. And while those policy makers may have good intentions, policies can also have unknown and unintended consequences if they fail to collect enough data, assess the impact of the policy, or fail to seek recommendations from subject matter experts. And that can lead to serious mistakes the decision-maker may not even be aware of, that could create systemic problems that produce other types of social problems.

An example of a policy that was highly motivated by the biases of lawmakers, and had very predictable negative consequences, were the get-trough-on-crime laws, and the mandatory sentencing laws, of the late '90s and early 2000s passed by many State governments in the United States. Ideally, lawmakers would pass laws and create programs aimed at reducing the burden of social problems on the community. For example, seeing an arrest as an opportunity to educate the offender on the problems of crime and, more importantly, provide inmates who reenter the community with better ways of living. When programs, like these, are effective and actually do something for the offender, it could potentially reduce crime and the burden on the community overtime. But in this instance, the negative biases of politicians towards criminal offenders made them blind to their negative economic consequences.

These laws basically increased sentences so that people with minor legal infractions where sometimes required to spend years, or decades, in prison. When you do the math, this solution puts an increasing burden on the State that exponentially grows worse overcome. Putting more people in prison, and increasing their sentences, is going to fill up

more prisons, redirect tax revenue from budgeted programs, and make it impossible for formerly incarcerated inmates to return to a normal life. So, lawmakers found themselves increasingly redirecting tax revenues away from fi-
nancing education, public safety, public infrastructure, and
programs aimed at reducing crime and poverty, to finance
the incarceration of inmates and build more prisons.

These laws were eventually overturned, but only after
the lawmakers saw the negative financial and social consequences nearly 15 years, after-the-fact. By 2014, Oklahoma,
a state that had adopted those laws, had one of the highest
incarceration rates in the U.S., and sadly, one of the highest
child homelessness rates in the nation. About 44 thousand
homeless children were living in temporary situations with
friends or family, many of which had parents who were incarcerated.[49]

When policies are based on intuition without looking at
the data or consulting with experts it can also have unintended consequences. With public infrastructure, for example, intuition may not be enough to judge the safety of a
bridge, or recognize structural deficiencies, as a trained
structural engineer would. Dong that could have prevented
the I-35 bridge collapsed during 2007 that killed more than
a dozen people and injured more than 140. Or consider the
Affordable Care Act (ACA), which was designed to make
sure people who have catastrophic conditions, like cancer,
have access to healthcare insurance in the United States.
While this act was well intended, it financial harmed many
of the people it was designed to help.

For example, a person working for an employer may pay
about $20 a month for healthcare insurance, with the em-
ployer paying the rest. And that insurance can be used to
get teeth cleaned, eyes checked, cover medical expenses for

treatments and medications, and receive annual checkups. But ACA insurance may cost $120 a month with a $5,000 deductible. What this meant is that the insurance company would not pay unless a medical bill exceeds $5,000. And at the beginning of the ACA, anyone who did not have insurance was required to get ACA insurance or face financial penalties.

So, some of the poorest people who could not afford insurance to begin with, were forced to pay for catastrophic insurance they could not use, unless their bill exceeded $5,000. An alternative to this would be to have the Federal government cover the cost of catastrophic conditions and use other financial instruments to cover the remaining costs. Doing that would reduce the excessive financial burdens on insurance companies and private individuals.

Policies should protect citizens and reduce instances of unfairness and injustice in society. But sometimes they do not go far enough. For example, if labor laws did a better job of protecting workers from the actions of corrupt managers, employers would have greater incentive to police their organizations and sanction abusive behavior. They may also be more incentivized to hire and promote qualified professionals, all of which creates greater fairness and equality in the labor market.

Consider At-Will employment laws that require an employee sign a contract stating that the employer can fire the employee for any reason. Laws like that protect business owners from frivolous lawsuits filed by employees who are motivated by monetary gain. But they also allow unscrupulous managers to fire people for no reason, even when the manager is at fault. The employer, in this situation, is not required to exercise a duty of care when investigating claims. In fact, Human Resources (HR) people may evaluate claims based on whether the business could be sued. And when they cannot, terminating the worker's employment may be easier than dealing with the problem. All they have to do is make-up a convincing lie to terminate the worker's employment. And that employee may be denied unemployment insurance as a result.

The problem with this, from a judgment perspective, is that the employer is automatically assumed to be operating responsibly, and the employee is automatically assumed to be at fault. And the employee, even in cases of wrongful termination lawsuits, may have no legal recourse. In the United States, workers who fall under the category of a federally protected class, like race, age, color, religion, sex, national origin, disability, genetic information, citizenship, or veteran status, may sue for wrongful termination, but only if they can prove the act was taken because of their classification. Otherwise, workers may have no legal protections.

Policy makers have many ways to reduce the negative consequences of policy decisions. More testing and scenario analysis could help policy makers understand the effectiveness and impact of a policy on different parts of the population. This could be done using data models that provide some idea of the social or economic consequences of a decision. Policies could be tried in pilot programs, on small representative parts of the population, to understand it's impact, and then scaled-out when problems in the model are resolved. Policy makers could collect more feedback from community involvement to allow citizens or businesses to report problems. And policy makers could learn from policies and programs that have succeeded or failed in increasing economic wealth, making communities safer, or making the population happier.

5
Responsible Use of Technology

People like to assume that computer technologies and artificial intelligence are purely objective and data-driven. In reality, those systems are designed and written by people who determine how those systems process and analyze information. How those systems are designed and written is based on the assumptions and mental logic of its designers and programmers. So, it is possible that human biases, bad logic, wrong assumptions, norms, and personal values, can be easily and intuitively baked into the programming logic of those applications by design to create systemic bias that unfairly judges and discriminates against people.

To give computers credit, automated computer systems are more trustworthy and fairer than humans. They won't steal from you, lie to you, and they generally treat people more fairly because they arrive at conclusions based on objective facts, rather than subjective beliefs or biases. Professionals and executives use them to inform their judgment by considering an incomprehensible amount of information. They are used by police and investigators to more quickly apprehend suspects. Health care professionals use them for faster and more accurate diagnosis, and for tracking diseases. And they are used by city planners to track population growth, plan public projects, and make decisions about where to invest in public infrastructure.

But data models can also be poorly designed by not including enough information to arrive at good conclusions. For example, a large distributer of Human Resources software recently released a product that would allow employers to predict whether an employee is likely to quit based on the number of jobs the candidate had, and how long the candidate stayed in those jobs. Employers using this software would then exclude a person who left previous jobs for reasons that have nothing to do with that person's performance.

People in official positions also try to wrongly apply statistical trends that occur in a sample, or population, to predicting an individual's behavior. For example, in at least nine states in the United States, software was used to help Judges assess the statistical risk factors of an offender repeating a crime when deciding a sentence.[5] In other words, rather than basing the sentence on the offender's own choices, that sentence is being partly based on the choices made by other people, who happen to makeup a statistical trend. Individuals will always be compelled to make choices that differ from the average.

6
Critical Skills

Social responsibility is all about understanding the impact your decisions have on your life, the lives of other people, or the environment. Ideally, you want to strive to have a positive impact. And you can do that by being more involved in community organizations, or by providing greater help and support to the people around you.

You also want to reduce the negative impact of your decisions. And you have a variety of tools for doing that. In a previous chapter, we looked at how you could do that using scenario analysis or reality testing to predict those consequences. You could also consult with an expert who may provide advice on your course of action. Or you could develop the expertise yourself by pursuing a more advanced level of education designed to give you the tools to avoid common predictable mistakes.

Powerful people can also have a tremendous positive or negative impact on people's lives. And the question is, do organizations allow powerful people to freely hurt and take advantage of others without consequences? This often happens in organizations that lack policies and policy enforcement, or within organizations that have policies, but do not enforce them. The solution to these problems, as we have already seen in previous chapters, may involve requiring people to answer for their decisions, and hold them accountable by attributing credit or blame for their decisions. When managers fail to hold people into account for the gains or losses that result from their decisions, it not only becomes difficult to predictably manage the business, it creates problems and unfairness for the employees that are never resolved. And that can result in high turnover rates, organizational disfunction, and other serious problems that reduce the efficiency and effectiveness of the organization, potentially to the point of bankruptcy.

Hold people accountable by not just pointing out mistakes, but by giving people credit when credit is deserved. First of all, you want to discourage people from causing you unnecessary harm or losses by drawing a line and sanctioning bad behavior. If you don't do that, then you are allowing people to cause you harm. You also want to encourage the input of people who are helpful by giving them credit for making things better.

Accountability is a basic management skill. Managers need to track workers and make judgments about who is making a positive or negative difference within the organization to make informed business decisions. When managers fail to do that, it allows people to repeatedly make terrible decisions that do significant harm or damage without consequences. Better accountability enables managers to promote people who are most capable of benefiting, and making valuable contributions to, the organization.

Improving human judgment enables us to reduce the negative impact decisions have on people's lives or the environment. But the problem of how we accomplish that task is something we will look at in the next part on assessing capabilities. One of the more practical and powerful tools available to us for overcoming the problems we face, involves developing human capabilities with practice and exercise. And many cause-and-effect relationships exist between human development and the resolution of human problems that many experts do not understand. And we look at many of those relationships in the next part on assessing capabilities.

Developing new abilities is our means for strengthening our overall condition, for improving mental health and performance of life roles, for helping people overcome the problems they face and obtain more of what they want, and for reducing many of the social problems that people face. In this next part, we look at the influence of human capabilities on motivation, in addition to how to extend human capabilities and further human potential.

PART III:
ASSESSING CAPABILITIES

The way people judge their abilities, and what they are capable of, certainly has an influence on their life goals. And, in many ways, you have more control over your own development than any other influencing factor on your condition. Similar to how software can be further developed by adding features and functionality, people can further develop their own abilities by adding new skills that change how they think and operate, to make them more effective in performing life roles.

Similar to writing a line of code, compiling it, and seeing the end-result, you can develop a habit or skill and put that skill into practice to see the end-result. For many people, developing specific skills or abilities can enable them to more effectively in solving life problems, gain more control over their future, improve their mental health, increase their income, and improve their life outcomes. And in the following chapters, we look at a number of ways in which personal development enables people to do that.

In this part of the book, we look at how behavioral change works, how to create new behaviors and new operational abilities by strengthening wanted responses that makeup habits and skills. The mind is like a muscle, in some ways, in that you can exercise by performing a task repeatedly and strengthen your ability to perform that task. Some people call these mind-building exercises as they tend to strengthen your mental capabilities to improve your mental fitness when performing a role. This applies to memory, and learning about a complex subject, to motor abilities, and more complex creative tasks.

In this next chapter, we look at how people assess their own condition and how that assessment influences their thinking and decisions. We look at the mental effects of capability, how it limits or expands human potential, and influences life goals. And we look at the mental effects of improving capability, and how it improves a person's overall condition. And in Chapter 6, we look at how those abilities actually develop, and the possibilities of shortening the development path.

CHAPTER 5:
THE HUMAN CONDITION

Your overall condition is comprised of the health, strength, and fitness of your mind and body, in addition to your social and financial status. And people, generally speaking, have the ability to strengthen and improve these different aspects of their overall condition. In this chapter, we look at some practical theories about how to improve the human condition. It looks at how that development limits or expands human potential, and translates into improved mental health and wellbeing.

Evidence presented in this book suggests that improving the mental health and the human condition is truly a combination of two factors. The first is personal development that improves a person's ability to perform roles and achieve goals. This can enable you to grow stronger, develop greater self-confidence, and have a better outlook on life. The second is reducing adversity that causes harm to the human condition and prevent beneficial growth and development. And we will look at why this is important in the last part of this book. Both of these together improve the self-confidence and resilience necessary to live a healthy life. But without hope and a positive outlook on life, created by life goals and a life purpose, especially if you are constantly faced with adversity, a person can become cornered and my fight back as we see with homicidal behaviors, like mass-shootings, or despairs and gives up as we see suicidal behaviors.

1
The Science of Behavior

If you watched a science fiction thriller in a movie theater recently, you may have found yourself sitting on the edge of your seat as the hero risks life-and-limb in death-defying acts of heroism. The suspense of not knowing whether the hero is capable enough, strong enough, or fast enough to make it out alive, keeps the audience enthralled with the hero's super-human abilities. And while you may not have super-human abilities yourself, you certainly have many strengths and core competencies that make you heroic in the eyes and minds of those who depend on you, like family, friends, or coworkers, by simply being there for them.

If a technology of the Human Sciences existed, it would certainly involve making people better, in some way, by further developing or enhancing human capability. All human behavior and responses arise from many types of human abilities, many of which are centrally governed by the ability of human judgment. They are like the features and functionality of the human machine that can be further developed or debugged. This is important because human abilities shape the modern world in many profound ways. Scientists could not cure diseases without the experts who make that possible. We could not have advanced transportation systems without engineers to design them. These are just a few examples in which human abilities limit or expand human potential.

As Human Scientists experiment with improving human capability, they will likely do it by using a few different approaches. The first involves studying and modifying human biology, like the brain, nervous system, muscular systems, and other anatomy that make-up the physical hardware and firmware of the human body. The second approach involves studying, or modifying, the behavior of that biology. Much of that behavior, especially when it is voluntary, is heavily influenced by human judgment, which directs behavior toward achieving biological, social, and financial ends.

Unlike biology, the behavior of that biology, is more abstract to study. You cannot take a behavior, pin-it-down, and study it under a microscope in a controlled laboratory setting the way you can with a human cell or DNA. You cannot ethically reproduce the long-term effects of child abuse using controlled laboratory experiments, primarily because people live with complex and unique set of personal and situational influences that could never be fully accounted for. So, to test a hypothesis, the Scientist cannot just go into the laboratory, test a theory, and get an immediate result the way you can with other sciences. This does not mean that behavior cannot be studied with the same scientific rigor and effectiveness as other subjects. But it does mean that testing a hypothesis may require months if not years of careful observation to determine whether it has merit.

Basic abilities can be directly quantitatively measured. In fact, grade-school teachers and college professors do it all the time with grading systems. If you can test for an ability, you can measure and improve that ability. Other abilities, on the other hand, may depend on better reporting of, and tracking the resolution to, problems. That may sound simple, but doing it effectively requires the scientist to operate more like a police detective when gathering and evaluating evidence. This is especially true when studying people's ability to overcome traumatic events, or develop healthy relationships, or a likable character. If you merely did a survey or questionnaire, you would only get a limited dataset of subjective experiences and opinions, rather than an expanded dataset of objective facts, like occupational status, income, crime-rate, sleep, consumption, and other contributing factors.

Genetics and biochemistry have a profound influence on human ability. People are often judged based on what they look like and sound like, which is largely influenced by genetics. A person's genetics can offer advantages, like height in basketball, physical attraction in modelling, or vocal abilities in music. So, people have some natural endowments that make them more suitable for performing certain roles. Some people call this "natural talent." But even if a professional athlete has a genetic advantage, that athlete still has to practice to be more competitive than an amateur.

Human abilities tend to have capacity, meaning that they can be further developed with practice and exercise. And the majority of the abilities required to live in the modern world does not come to people fully developed. They have to be tested, strengthened, and improved, which is the programming logic of human behavior. At a low-level, that development begins with the nervous system, which enables the brain to build models and simulations, upon which people form judgments and make decisions. At a higher level, it continues by developing intellectual abilities, which depend on the acquisition and use of knowledge. Both of these inform judgment and motivate behavior.

2
Consequential Abilities

Human motives tend to be highly goal oriented as people try to fulfill biological goals for safety and nourishment, or more complex social goals for money and relationships. And the abilities that makeup behavior are highly consequential because they are the means to achieving those goals. So, the more a person can strengthen those abilities, the more effective and successful that person can be in achieving those goals.

Abilities often develop adaptively in response to environmental demands. Anytime you are put into a new environment, whether it is a website, a transit system, or an office building, you are forced to learn how to navigate that environment. You meet new people, learn new names and places, perform new tasks and jobs, and follow new rules and guidelines. If you find yourself in a dangerous part of town and you frequently worry about being victimized by a criminal, you have greater motivation and incentive to develop habits around personal protection, like locking doors, being suspicious of strangers, and carrying a weapon. Different circumstances, elicit different responses, and give rise to different behaviors.

Human abilities are the human causes of success and failure in projects. The success of all human endeavors is conditional, and contingent, upon the existence of specific abilities. So, understanding why abilities develop, why they fail to develop, how they improve, their economic value, their effects on thought processes and emotional states, and their consequences, can enable people to be more successful in their endeavors. If you are in a situation in which you need to perform a task or solve a problem, like creating a water well in the middle of the desert, and you do not know how, then you will leave yourself worse-off. So, possessing specific abilities can improve outcomes, and knowledge-deficits or skills-deficits can make outcomes worse.

Knowing that developing certain abilities can make your situation better off, can give you greater responsibility for the course of your life. But it also means that lacking certain skills or abilities can make a person less responsible for one's future, for example, when a person lacks knowledge of what to do.

These basic ideas also apply to organizational management, and understanding the human capital required to make the organization effective and efficient enough to remain profitable. When managers or workers lack the training required to perform work and meet management expectations, the organization suffers. So, understanding the cause-and-effect relationship between human ability and achieving goals is vital to the success of any human effort.

3
Mindsets and the Effects of Discouragement

During the last century, many studies have demonstrated that how people judge their own abilities can have a profound influence on the way they judge themselves, their self-worth, and their potential. For example, having the ability to do something improves your confidence in success. Without that ability, you have more reason to be discouraged and give-up. Self-confidence, by itself, is not a determinant of mental health, or an indicator of whether a person has severe mental disorders. Rather, it is more of an indicator, or symptom, of mental health. People actually improve their condition by strengthening targeted skills and abilities, the biproduct of which tends to be improved self-confidence. In later parts of this book, we look at how adversity, rather than self-confidence, has more of a profound effect on a person's mental health.

But a person's beliefs about one's own abilities can influence that person's development and life goals. Psychologist Carol Dweck explored this idea in her book *Mindset: The New Psychology of Success,* in which she shows how people's beliefs have an influence on human development. To demonstrate this, she presents two different mindsets: 1) A fixed mindset, which views intelligence as fixed and limited; and 2) a growth mindset, which views intelligence as capable of further growth and development.[15]

A person with a fixed mindset, according to Dweck, believes that intelligence and talent are fixed traits that people are born with. This is similar to a belief that people are genetically programmed biological robots who are born with fixed traits. The fixed mindset views a person's intelligence as unchanging and incapable of improvement. This means that people who are born smart do not have to work as hard, intellectually, as a person who is not born smart. So, a person with a fixed mindset may be more discouraged from taking on difficult or challenging tasks to avoid failure and embarrassment. That person may also have more incentive to lie to coverup shortcomings in one's abilities, or cheat to get ahead. To a person with a fixed mindset, these strategies appear necessary since one is at a disadvantage in comparison to smarter people.

In contrast, a person with a growth mindset sees intelligence and talent as capable of change and improvement with effort and persistence. To a person with a growth mindset, failure does not mean that person was not smart enough, but rather not enough time and effort was put into achieving the end result. Instead of fearing failure, a person with a growth mindset may welcome challenges that provide the opportunity for new growth and development. A person with a growth mindset gets ahead, not because that person was born smarter, but because that person works harder, and strengthens their abilities by putting their abilities to the challenge. This mindset tends to be more encouraging, and could enable a person to be more resilient during difficult times, and more capable of overcoming rejection and failure.

Dweck's concept of mindsets is instrumental for demonstrating how people's beliefs in their abilities, and what they are capable of doing, influences their life-altering choices. An example of this, according to Dweck, is when a fixed mindset person is discouraged from learning and drops out of a challenging academic course as a result of not being smart enough. A student with a growth mindset, in contrast, may view the same subject as a worthy challenge that only becomes difficult as a result of not studying. People only exert effort when they believe it will pay-off. And when a person does not believe it will pay-off, then one has no reason to try.

Beliefs about abilities also influences personal treatment. An instructor with a fixed mindset may only help students who appear to be smart enough, and lose patience or give-up on students who are not. Parents with a fixed mindset may only help specific children who appear to have potential and give-up on those who do not. Or in the business world, a fixed mindset manager may look for workers who are smart, and perform at a high level on the first day, rather than relying on coaching and training. That also means that the fixed mindset manager is less responsible for the direction of the organization and more likely to put the blame for organizational failures on market forces, like a lack of talent in the labor market.

In the final part of this book, we look at how adversity can have a much more profound negative effect on a person's mental state and development, than a lack of skills or a lack of self-confidence. But it also has developmental implications. For example, repeated verbal discouragement by telling a child that she or he will never amount to anything, could cause a lack self-confidence later in life. That could not only demotivate the child, and influence the child to avoid trying, it could cause that person to make less-than-desirable life choices, like avoiding opportunities that would lead to better life outcomes. And those failures may lead to more failure and more rejection. And the question arises, when a person lacks confidence in one's ability to achieve goals legitimately, does that person feel the need to lie, cheat, and hurt others, to get ahead?

Life circumstances can also be discouraging. For example, when a person is in a miserable situation and perceives a lack of control over life, that person may be less likely to do anything about it and may become depressed. A child who is unable to escape the daily mistreatment of an abusive parent may learn to live with the mistreatment, which can have a detrimental effect on the child's mental health overtime. Or when a person is trapped in an unsatisfying job or a miserable relationship, and feels helpless to do anything about it, the person may be more likely to give up and accept a miserable state of affairs. When a person stops trying as a result of discouragement, or feeling helpless, that can be a symptom of depression.

4

Developmental Solutions

Human problems have many causes, some of which can be biological and may require surgery or medications to resolve. But some problems are developmental, meaning the person, for whatever reason, failed to develop healthy abilities, habits, or skills, that enable them to have a sense of self-confidence and be resilient during difficult times. And while many developmental problems are sometimes treated with medications or punishment, a more effective, longer-term, approach is to apply a developmental solution.

Developmental solutions, which are solutions to life problems that involve developing targeted abilities, have their strengths and weaknesses. Not all problems are resolvable using developmental programs. And not all developmental programs are effective, especially when they do not factor in the cause-and-effect relationships required to make them successful. Developmental programs also require time and effort, sometimes taking weeks, months, or years before you see results. But the advantage is that those results tend to be longer-lasting, more permanent, and sometimes life-changing.

The purpose of developing specific skills or abilities is that they solve problems of everyday living. For example, a lack of social skills, conflict resolution skills, or communication skills, tends to cause problems in personal relationships. A lack of healthy lifestyle habits can lead to health-related problems later in life. And a lack of exercise or training in your different life roles could cause your mental fitness to decline.

Maintaining health and fitness can also be a use-it or

114

lose-it proposition. Abilities that are not regularly exercised, repeatedly challenged, reinforced, and strengthened, tend to grow weaker, atrophy, and waste away. By challenging and strengthening your life skills, you improve your ability to handle life's demands, overcome situational challenges, improve performance fitness, and improve your ability to achieve goals. The self-confidence you gain from stronger skills can make you more resilient during difficult, stressful, and discouraging times. The practice of learning, by itself, can improve attention and comprehension, stimulate brain growth and strengthen neural connections. Active engagement in learning about a subject you have an interest or passion in, may have a reenergize and renewing effect on your overall mental state. And eating a healthier diet and engaging in regular physical or mental activity can improve brain function as a result of improved body composition and improved circulation of oxygen and nutrients.

If researchers could identify the developmental deficits that cause social problems, it may be possible to formulate better developmental programs to combat those problems. For example, many abilities fail to develop because of inexperience, lacking self-confidence, severe adverse experiences, a lack of opportunity, a physical or mental limitation, or other causes. Adversity can be particularly discouraging. Significant amounts of childhood adversity are known to cause problems with cognitive development, educational attainment, problems forming healthy relationships, and problems regulating emotions. All of these problems lead to poorer choices later in life.

The problem with creating effective developmental programs, like training programs or rehabilitation programs, is that they may not effective when they are first created, which is one of the main reasons they fail. Creating an effective developmental program takes time because it requires you to look at it as a technology that can be built-on and innovated with science. For example, when a program is initially created, some methods will work and others will not. If you have two identical programs, and you are tracking the progress of participants, and one program requires classroom training, and the other requires personal interaction, which participants from which programs do better in the long run? You can answer that question using your intuition. But if you let the numbers do the talking, the program will become increasingly more effective overtime. Programs, like these, could then be shared with other researchers, who can contribute their own discoveries to create better, and more effective, programs.

5

Critical Skills

A direct relationship exists between your abilities and your success or failure in performing roles or achieving goals. Beliefs about what you are capable of doing can also limit or expand your potential. If you believe you cannot do something, you are less likely to try, and you are more likely to fail and give-up. Or just as bad, you may resort to dishonesty or cheating to get ahead.

To avoid these problems, learn to like challenges, similar to how a gamer likes to play video games. If you like to challenge your abilities and solve problems, you will more eager to learn and develop, and may develop greater optimism, resilience, grit, and persistence to push through difficult times. Personal development also requires patience and time commitment. If you are not willing to schedule time for personal development, it may be difficult to be successful in the ways you want.

If you want to be more successful in an endeavor, you could try to identify weak areas or knowledge deficits that may contribute to failure, and strengthen those abilities. Once you identify areas needing improvement, you can establish small, well-defined, goals for your development, and regularly work toward those goals with routines and regimens. Even if it's only thirty minutes a day, those routines can help you to improve your social life, skills development, and physical exercise. In your social life, you may consider what would you like to do that you have never done before? Or, in your skills development, consider the weaknesses or deficits that cause you the most problems in your work life? Active engagement in learning about interests and passions can have a reenergizing effect on your mental state and improve your overall self-confidence.

This chapter briefly looked at practical theories about what causes the human condition to improve or decline. The problem is, developing healthy habits and skills may seem easy and intuitive, since all you need is practice and exercise. But people are not always successful in doing that for many reasons. And in the next chapter, we look at some reasons why people fail, and techniques for reducing the amount of time required to develop skills.

CHAPTER 6:
SKILLS DEVELOPMENT

If personal development is so easy and intuitive, you have to wonder why people frequently fail in this endeavor. Knowing how to effectively develop new skills and abilities, beyond what you learning in the classroom in grade school, can give you greater control over the course of your life. You can do a better job at preparing yourself, and improving your fitness, for performing life roles. But to do that effectively, you need to measure your progress and be capable of understanding your progress in an objective way.

Skills development is also fundamental to behavioral change because you are essentially changing the way a person operates by extending or further developing their abilities. Much of this development may apply to your core competencies, which includes knowledge and skills that you are highly specialized in, and is typically related to your life roles, like your occupation or profession. By strengthening your core competencies, you not only improve your ability to perform professional roles, you can also improve your earnings potential.

These techniques can be used to develop talent within organizations as well, to make organizations more effective in achieving its goals. Our civilization's ability to master the techniques of skills development will determine how quickly we solve problems, how successful we are as a people, and how far we technologically advance.

1

The Principle of Gradual Improvement

One of the reasons people fail in their personal development has to do with the way they develop their abilities. Almost all personal development, whether you are developing a habit, a skill, or a talent, follows the *Principle of Gradual Improvement*, which suggests that the more you work to overcome the limitations in an ability, the stronger that ability becomes. When you think about it, encoding a memory or an ability requires a first attempt. If you fail in that first attempt, you may continue making attempts until you are successful. This process of encoding new knowledge and abilities requires time and effort.

Practice does make improvement. If you ask any bodybuilder or athlete for advice on how to become stronger at doing something, they may tell you "it's all in the reps" (i.e., the repetitions). In other words, you have to do that activity frequently. And you have to focus on, and frequently revisit, specific areas of development in which you are weak. If you spend too little time developing an ability, either you will not develop that ability at all, or your performance will suffer.

Intuitively, it appears that the more you do something, the better you get. The more you practice, reflect on, and finetune an ability, the stronger that ability becomes. The greater number of times you practice remembering something, the stronger that memory becomes, which improves your fitness in performing that task. Or, the more conversations you have, the more questions you think of and the more topics you talk about.

K. Anders Ericsson, who spent more than 30 years researching the subject of expertise says, in his book *Peak: Secrets from the New Science of Expertise*, that repetition only goes so far to improve an ability. He makes the case that simply because someone has performed a task, repeatedly, for many years does not necessarily make that person better overtime.[16] For example, an amateur tennis player, he explained, may be good enough to play against other players. But his skills eventually plateau and stop improving. In fact, his skills may eventually decline as a result of forgetting. The root of the problem, he says, is that people get comfortable in their occupational roles, develop automated routines, and stop learning and developing in new ways, especially when they are not required. What influences the development of expertise the most, according to Ericsson's research, is the amount of work put into improving that expertise. And, specifically, people make the most progress when they are laser-focused on strengthening weak abilities. The problem is, people often do not know where their weaknesses are.

One way to identify your weaknesses is by seeking expert guidance, which can accelerate the learning process and rapidly improve your skills development. For instance, a skill that would take you a year to develop as a result of figuring things out, or from trail-and-error, or from learning from mistakes, may only take you a week or a month to develop under the guidance of an expert who has already learned from those mistakes and can provide you with beneficial feedback.

If you really want to develop your skills, according to Ericsson, perform a task that requires more effort and causes you to make mistakes. When you learn something new, you are forced to face your lack of knowledge. And that forces your brain to exert extra effort to change and adapt. This gives you the opportunity to recognize weaknesses, and then learn and strengthen those abilities with practice and persistence. If you only remain in your comfort zone and perform tasks you are already good at, you will not develop any further in your existing abilities no matter how many years you do it.

2
Habits

A *habit* is a response to routine circumstances that becomes more automatic with repetition. Habits tend to be so automatic, and so ingrained into your behavioral and thinking patterns, that people tend to default back to habits when making important life decisions. This is one of the reasons why habits are so powerful and why they can override your better judgment. But habits can also be beneficial and rewarding, for example, if you have strong habits of practice and exercise that enables you to develop the skills necessary to be successful in performing a task. The trick to habit formation is learning how responses become encoded into memory and habituated, and how the brain forges new neural pathways and establishes new methods of operating.

If you want to develop a new habit then, according to researchers, you may want to stick to a regimen. For example, if you want to develop a daily habit of practicing a new skill, you could start by scheduling the same time every day to practice that skill. In the *Power of Habit: Why We Do What*

We Do in Life and Business, New York Times journalist
Charles Duhigg explores the science and applications of
habits in a variety of different subjects including neurology,
business, marketing, and sports. In the first chapter, he explores the structure of a habit, as identified by MIT researchers, and how habits are triggered by cues, like environmental cues.[14] Deciding what to eat for lunch because it's noon
time, or deciding to wash hands because they are dirty, are
examples of habits triggered by environmental cues.

People sometimes fail to establish new habits because
they make the activity more difficult and stressful than it
needs to be, which can be discouraging. For example, if you
want to develop better exercise habits, it's better to start
within your comfort zone and gradually increase the level
of difficulty. Even if you are only within your comfort zone,
establishing the routine is the most important part of developing a habit. So, if you start by making the exercise too
strenuous or difficult, and leave yourself in pain, or worse
discouraged, you may be demotivating yourself from doing
it again. The age-old wisdom "no pain, no gain" absolutely
contains a nugget of truth. But you need to be successful in
establishing the habit, first, by associating the activity with
a scheduled time (i.e., the environmental cue), before you
can go on to bigger and better successes. Focusing on establishing the habit first also enables you to make it more enjoyable so that you will want to pursue and engage in that
activity more frequently. If you decide you want to become
more competitive, then you can simply increase the intensity and become more laser focused on overcoming your
weaknesses.

Habits also differ by complexity. Buckling your seatbelt
is a habit that requires one step. But preparing a meal is

more complex and requires many steps. Even with additional complexity, it can be habituated with practice and repetition. As a task is performed repeatedly, and the response becomes encoded into the neural pathways of the brain, the amount of mental effort required to perform that task decreases, which is known as habituation.

Habits dictate many daily behaviors. You have dietary consumption habits, hygiene habits, like brushing teeth, and physical activity habits, which may contribute to a healthy or unhealthy lifestyle. You have habits in terms of your emotional attitudes in the way you respond to other people and circumstances. You have social habits in the way you introduce yourself and whether you are polite. You have purchasing habits in the way you budget and spend your money. And you have work habits in how you perform your work.

All of these habits influence your personality and character. In the minds of your coworkers, you become the type of person who shows up early to work. And it's not that you are a static, unchanging, type of person, but that you have well-established habits, routines, and behavioral patterns, that have become your dominant traits. As you have a stronger inclination, and a stronger habit, to respond in specific ways, those dominant traits become more prominently expressed overtime, giving you a very distinctive personality and character.

Because habits influence your daily life so much, the goal of many behavioral change programs tends to focus on getting rid of old habits, or substituting an old habit with a new habit. The problem with doing that, is that old habits do not die easily. They are deeply rooted and have established neural connections that remain, even if you wanted them to disappear, and could take years if not decades to atrophy and be forgotten. If habits were like flowers in a garden, it's not possible to simply reach into your brain and uproot an old habit. You have to plant new habits, and forge new neural pathways, and let the old ones die with disuse.

The second problem is that developing a new habit is not always a process of flipping a switch. You may have to learn a new skill. It would be convenient to be able to substitute an unhealthy choice with a healthy choice. But the reason that may not be possible is that a healthy choice requires learning about healthy food, healthy ingredients, learning how to prepare a healthy meal, or learning where to buy a healthy meal. And most importantly, you want to eat healthy meals that are delicious and satisfying. No matter how healthy the food is, if it is not delicious and satisfying, then why would you continue eating it? If you do not figure that out, and do not figure out where to buy healthy food, or how to make it, your food will never be delicious or satisfying enough. And consequently, you will end-up at the fast-food drive-thru eating junk food and crying into your soda-pop over your unhealthy habits.

Behavioral change requires more than changing daily routines and habits. It may require learning and training. For example, if you want to learn about healthier dietary choices, you may start by learning about what foods and ingredients are healthy or unhealthy. You may also want to learn how to balance the calories you consume with the calories required for performing daily activities. And that knowledge reinforces healthy behaviors and guides your thinking in the right direction. But secondly, you need to learn where to buy healthy food, or how to make it, or you will never change. And that requires skills development. For someone wanting to lose a little weight, skills development can be more effective and permanent than surgery, medications, or incentive systems, because it actually changes the behavior that created the problem to begin with.

3
Skills

A *skill* is an ability that can be further developed with effort, practice, and exercise. It could be a motor skill, like shooting an arrow, or an intellectual skill, like solving mathematical problems. A skill is like a mind muscle that grows stronger or weaker depending on use or disuse. Similar to how the human body can be more physically fit to perform physical activities, the brain can be more mentally fit to perform specific life roles. Each role you perform can be broken down into a number of abilities, like speaking, communication, or technical abilities. And when one of those abilities has capacity for improvement, we call that a skill.

Skills can potentially increase your self-esteem, or how you evaluate your abilities and contributions. For example, if you are a beginner at playing a game and do not perform well, other players may not have a high evaluation of your skills. If you perform at a high level and win most of the points for the team, you can become a highly valued player. As you improve your skills, you may also improve how people judge you, and the value they place in your skills, which could positively influence your relationships.

When skills have monetary exchange value, they are sometimes called human capital. Since people cannot be experts in everything, when a problem arises, they hire people to perform work for them. If you are not an expert, and you need a home appliance repaired or vehicle repaired, you may hire someone to perform that work for you, to save time and hassle. In this instance, the repair person's occupational or professional skills have monetary value that enables one to earn a living and financially support oneself.

Skills can also improve judgment and decision-making. Since the expert tends to have a better mental model of how a system works, that expert is more capable of recognizing predictable mistakes and preventing negative consequences. This is one of the reason companies pay more money to employ skilled and qualified professionals. Those professionals already know solutions to difficult problems and do not have to spend time and money learning from trial-and-error mistakes, which can improve efficiency and the effectiveness of the organization well enough to remain profitable.

Imagine if a medical doctor or a construction engineer did not have adequate training. The consequences could be catastrophic. You could have people die from infections, or you could have a building sink into the ground, catch on fire, and kill everyone inside, because of incompetence and malpractice. Hiring someone who is fully trained and qualified, who understands the resource requirements, is able to predict the causes of failure and complete a job in a predictable and reasonable amount of time. That can save a considerable amount of money in comparison to hiring a less skilled worker at a lower cost. But, despite facing serious consequences, many employers still underestimate the skills require to perform the work. That is especially true in Information Technology where, according to a Harris Poll conducted in 2020, 38% of state and local government employees said that they were not trained in ransomware prevention. This comes after more than 100 cities across the United States were attacked by ransomware the previous year in 2019.[47]

The economic factors of production tend to include things, like time, labor, or materials, necessary to produce a good or service. The human factors, which include labor, human capital, and know-how, can be more critical to determining the success or failure than any other factor. A failure in any human factor of production, like a lack of skills or know-how, can drive up costs, cause budget overruns as a result of incorrect estimates, require additional help as a result of lacking the expertise to perform a task, or cause the project to fail.

4

Role Skills

In William Shakespeare's play *As You Like It*, Jaques says "All the world's a stage, and all the men and women merely players; they have their exits and their entrances; and one man in his time plays many parts." This statement is also true in life, whether you are a parent, employee, business owner, or leader. You play many roles defined by many different skillsets.

Role skills can improve your ability to perform a role effectively. And you have many different ways of learning those skills, including role modeling, instruction, and expert advice, all of which can save considerable time that would be wasted learning the hard-way, or using a trial-and-error approach, and potentially giving up in failure. A role model can be instrumental in helping you learn the skills required to perform a role, especially if you have a great role model who is helpful and provides positive feedback and encouragement. And professional training and instruction can accelerate the development of professional skills.

Strong parenting skills can dramatically improve outcomes for both the parent and the child, and can influence the child's future in many ways. When parents lack strong parenting skills, they may be more likely to abuse or neglect their child, or attempt to punish the child into submission by using threats, or bribe the child with money. Children who experience significant adversity because of their caregiver's lack of parenting skills, may develop behavioral problems and lack social skills that lead to other problems.

Providing encouragement, and encouraging a child to try a challenging, but achievable, tasks is a parenting skill. Those challenges may involve personal interaction, learning, or problem solving, to enable the child to be more capable, confident, and mentally prepared to take-on similar challenges. Encouraging a child to seek out challenges, not only strengthens that child's abilities, the child will build the courage and self-confidence required to take-on other types of life challenges and achieve goals. And that can translate into maturing into a healthy and independent adult.

Management skills within organizations are similar in that they can dramatically improve the organization's ability to achieve its goals. Those skills may include personal skills, communication skills, leadership skills, the ability to manage costs, identify competitive advantages, or determine optimal pricing. Lacking basic management skills can ruin a business by introducing inefficiencies, lost revenues, negligence, and faulty practices. When management lacks strong leadership skills, it can cause a decline in worker productivity, a perception of unfairness among workers, employee turnover, conflict that reduces cooperation, and a decline in sales.

Managers who lack leadership skills often try to motivate worker performance by threat or intimidation. And while those negative consequences are short-term motivators, it tends to motivate dishonesty among workers to avoid negative consequences, or seek employment elsewhere, which causes turnover. Alternatively, managers could increase worker productivity by encouraging higher performance and skills development, giving workers credit for their contributions, holding them accountable for their mistakes, and monitoring the quality of production. Most workers want to perform their work well but sometimes do not understand the employer's expectations. So, correcting some mistakes may only require guidance or training. Giving workers praise and gratitude for certain types of contributions recognizes their work, which can encourage them to produce better work, and will improve worker retention by increasing their commitment to the organization.

5

Character Development

Character is a unique collection of personal qualities and characteristics that includes your personality, reputation, and personal history. In science fiction movies and television shows, characters are often exaggerated into superheroes or evil villains, depending on their role and how they are characterized. But in real life, a person's character may consist of one's occupation, life achievements, hobbies, and social disposition.

Character development can be instrumental in guiding your development and productivity by establishing goals for who you aspire to be. A husband may aspire to be a family man, a handy man, a man of faith, or may help friends or family. Or maybe you may want to become a better expert, or develop a track record of success. All of these personal characteristics and attributes go into building your character.

Part of what influences character are the principles people follow. Think of principles as the rules for behavior that people create to prevent themselves from getting into trouble. For example, a person may live by the principle of abstaining from alcoholic drinks. Or, if a person does drink, that person may have no more than one drink an hour to avoid getting drunk in public.

Character also plays an integral part in the development of personal relationships. When considering whether a person is suitable for a role as a spouse or an employee, the focus is often on character because people want a person with a certain character for the role. Suppose a hiring manager is choosing between two candidates for a management position. One candidate has wild behavior and the other candidate is well-behaved and professional. The hiring manager may prefer the more professional candidate because of how that person represents the business when interacting with workers and clients.

But character can also be deceptive. This is true when a person lies about one's identity, professional accomplishments, or financial condition, because that person wants to appear to have a track record of success. Job candidates may lie about their achievements and expertise to gain a higher-paying employment position. Or a manager may forge a fake character, consisting of a charming and sophisticated personality, but may lack the skills required to adequately perform that role. Con-artists (i.e., confidence artists) often use this tactic when trying to convince unsuspecting people to hand over their money for illicit purposes.

6

The Learning Curve

The learning curve is the amount of time, effort, and knowledge required to learn a new skill or subject. Every new behavior or skill, whether it involves performing a task or learning the core concepts of a subject, has a learning curve. A learning curve can be short, like learning a simple motor skill, or it can be very long and complex, like making through medical school. Learning curves can be applied to expertise and knowledge accumulation, or performance and efficiency gains from repeating a task.

One of the earliest references to the learning curve comes from the 1880's from Psychologist Hermann Ebbinghaus who used it to represent proficiency and the rate at which a person learns a subject. In Hermann's model, the vertical Y-axis represents proficiency and the horizontal X-axis represents the time spent learning. Starting at zero, a person's proficiency and knowledge increases as the amount of time spent learning increases. This graph represents knowledge accumulation over a period of time.

During later decades, Theodore P. Wright, in his 1936 book *Factors Affecting the Cost of Airplanes,* applied the learning curve to Management Science. Wright's version was different in that it did not focus on expertise but, instead, on the rate of production. In Write's model, the vertical Y-axis represents the average time (or labor cost) required to produce a unit of product, and the horizontal X-axis represents the cumulative volume of production. When the volume of production is zero, the average time required to produce a unit is high. And the amount of time required to produce each additional unit decreases. This graph represents the efficiency and performance gains made from repeating a task.

To illustrate Write's model, imagine you are hired to assemble chairs at a furniture manufacturer. When you assemble your first chair, you have to think through each step, or maybe ask questions, so you do not make a mistake during assembly. As you assemble each additional unit, each step is sequenced in memory so that the amount of time it takes to produce each additional unit decreases, maybe from 10 minutes to 3 minutes. The more your brain sequences the steps to perform the task, and the faster your brain is able to step through that sequence, it becomes increasingly more automatic and habituated.

People learn at different rates. But it may be possible to shorten the learning curve, depending on how a subject is presented. At a grade-school level, if a subject is made unnecessarily complex, it could overwhelm and discourage some students, and motivate them to cheat, or take shortcuts, to get ahead. On the other hand, if the learning materials do a better job at simplifying complex concepts, and only provides the minimum viable path with concise definitions and simple workflows, it may be possible for students to get over the learning curve faster and move on to more advanced topics. New technologies, like online videos, search engines, and digital instructors, may also provide additional learning resources. Ideally, subject matter experts should be able to test and evaluate different approaches to find the optimal approach for each subject.

7

Confidence Assessment

Self-confidence, in this book, is defined as confidence in

your abilities. And having confidence in your abilities can help to drive success. Anyone can learn or try and should have a basic sense of self-confidence in those basic abilities. Self-confidence can help you be resilient in the face of adversity because it's encouraging and enables you to overcome your vulnerabilities to criticism, failure, and loss, to solve problems and achieve the goals. In fact, to do just about anything, you need a basic sense of confidence in your ability to be successful, or you would not even try. The encouraging effect of self-confidence could be called the confidence effect.

A colleague of mine told me about his son who took up skydiving. At first, he was terrified and did not know that he could bring himself to do it. But after his first attempt, skydiving became his new favorite pastime. Sometimes people only know they are able to do something after they have pushed themselves to do it. This is why grit, itself, comes from more than encouragement, it comes from previous experience and having pushed yourself beyond your limits. From those experiences, you learn how to consistently push yourself to produce better results.

Strong judgment, when it comes to assessing your own abilities, requires you to question your judgment and get accurate feedback about your performance. And because of that, self-doubt is not always negative feedback. If you need to perform at a high level, but are not confident in your ability to perform at that level, your self-doubt can motivate you to train harder to strengthen your weaknesses. If you lack that self-doubt, either out of ignorance or because of previous successes, that false sense of self-confidence may prevent you from being motivated enough to succeed.

Subjective self-confidence, or subjective self-doubt, is not the most accurate or objective way to judge your own performance. In fact, subjective confidence is notorious for cause over-confidence or under-confidence that causes people to make mistakes. And later in this chapter, we look at how measuring ability provides more objective feedback about performance.

Under-confidence and over-confidence are forms of poor judgment, or instances in which your judgment is biased, and may lead to mistakes or failure. When people are not confident enough in their ability to do something, they often try to avoid it. And that becomes a problem when a person starts avoiding the simplest challenges. The challenges people face in life are not always complicated or difficult. Sometimes they merely require a person to try, to put in effort, and invest the time. And if you do not do that because of under-confidence, you will not develop in the ways you want, you will not build the life that you want, and will always be dissatisfied.

In contrast, some people are too confident in their ability to succeed, which sets them up for failure. Over-confidence means that you are so confident in your abilities and conclusions that you are not questioning the soundness of your judgment to correct your error. People have many reasons for their over-confidence. They may establish unrealistic goals without considering the amount of time and effort required to achieve those goals. Or when a person is successful at one thing, that person begins to believe that success can transfer to other endeavors as well.

8

Measuring Ability

Under-confidence and over-confidence are a problem because those judgments are based on subjective beliefs about one's performance. But, if that judgment could be based on objective results, those measurements could provide a more accurate and unbiased assessment of your performance.

A goal of many scientists involves quantifying the subject using measurable units because it makes it easier to study the subject and work it with objectively. Chemists measure the mass of atoms and molecules using mass spectrometry, Physicists measure gravitational fields, and Biologists measure cellular structures. But how is behavior measured? If we wanted to quantify an ability to objectively study function, operation, or performance, how would that work?

In behavior science, an ability is a fundamental unit of behavior that can be defined, tested, measured, analyzed, and sometimes improved. Anytime you can test an ability, you can potentially measure and improve that ability. This is how we move from a subjective opinion, or bias, of a person's development, to an objective measurement.

If you think about the human body as a type of machine, it would consist of different parts, each having their own abilities, that operate together to bring about end results. Each ability is like a feature that defines how people operate and what they are capable of doing. Some of those features are static and unchanging, like eye sight or hearing, and other features can be further developed with learning or training. By understanding how these abilities develop, why they fail to develop, how they influence thought processes, and how they improve people's ability to perform life roles, people are able to be more effective in achieving their goals.

Skills and abilities, as we have seen previously, tend to solve basic problems of living and enable people to achieve basic life goals, like acquiring the basic necessities of living, or how to solve a more complex social or financial problems. In fact, many of our most important life skills that enable people to be good citizens, employees, parents, or leaders do not come to us naturally. They have to be developed with effort and practice. To solve those problems or achieve those goals, people need to know how to effectively develop those skills.

This problem with "effectively developing skills" is that people need to assess the strength of their skills. Since intuition is people's default mode of thinking, much of their self-assessment is a matter of their opinion, which is susceptible to mistakes. The only way to measure the strength of a skill, to see objective results rather than subjective beliefs, is by quantifying those results.

Testing an ability, allows you to measure, and obtain objective feedback about, the strength of an ability. Without quantitative feedback, you only have a subjective opinion to form an assessment, which may be very inaccurate and prone to overconfidence. If you are trying to improve your golf game and you base your progress on your beliefs, without actually looking at the score, you may have a false sense of confidence in your abilities. Objective and numeric feedback prevents you from thinking you are making more progress than you really are, and allows you to get a more realistic assessment of your competitiveness.

If Susan wants to be a competitive athlete, but only applies the strategy of trying her best, which is highly subjective, she will probably lose. To be competitive with other athletes, she needs to test, measure, and compare her performance with those of other athletes. That test will tell her where her weaknesses are, what she needs to spend time on, and what activities she needs to schedule to strengthen those specific weaknesses.

Human abilities can be tested and measured in many different ways. Most people are familiar with academic learning, using test scores, grading systems, and averages. And it's certainly possible to measure a person's knowledge of a subject, ability to complete a task, perform a role, or any other task that has a success or failure result, based on objective criteria. Technology may also provide several different ways of measuring abilities using computer aided technologies, mobile apps, or more advanced technologies, like Functional Magnetic Resonance Imaging (fMRI) scans. Even general abilities, like human judgment, could be measured using a variety of academic or interactive tests. For example, some law enforcement agencies use virtual reality to train police officers. The goal of the virtual training is to test the officer's ability to use good judgment, and use the right skills, in high-pressure situations that sometimes cause officers to make mistakes.

Some abilities are more difficult to test, like a person's ability to attract a mate. And some tests are more effective than others, depending on how objective the criteria and results are. For example, a Scientist may look only for evidence supporting one's hypothesis and exclude evidence that does not, which is sometimes called a confirmation bias. But whether you are developing a new skill, a scientist creating a developmental program, or a manager creating a training program, using the most objective criteria possible will go far in generating the least biased results.

9

Skills Tests

A *skills test* is a test of whether a person or organization possesses an ability required to perform a task or achieve a goal. The process of developing a skill begins with a test and observing the result. The first time you try something, you may fail. But as you test your skills, and observe or measure the strength of those skills, you gradually figure out how to overcome your weaknesses and build confidence in your ability to do it again. Overtime, your successes or failures provide feedback on how much confidence you should have in that skill and whether you need to continue developing it or stop wasting your time.

Different skills require different tests. Testing for an intellectual ability, like mathematical proficiency, is a relatively simple academic exercise. Traditional Intelligence Quotient (IQ) tests attempt to measure and score general intelligence. But in recent decades, Psychologists have moved away from the idea of general intelligence, and have focused on specific types of intellectual abilities, like visual intelligence or emotional intelligence, which may be improved depending on the amount of time and effort invested into those specific skills.

Confidence plays a fundamental role in driving your success. But subjective confidence alone is not enough to be successful. If you have a false sense of self-confidence in your ability to do something, you are more likely to fail. It's not uncommon for someone to underestimate the skill required to perform a task, like hitting the bullseye with a bow and arrow. But until you actually try and succeed on a consistent basis, you have no idea how you will actually perform. Testing and objectively measuring your skills can give you a more honest assessment of your performance fitness and the strength of your condition.

Suppose Tim proudly tells his coworkers he is going to run the upcoming marathon. A few days before the marathon, he decides to practice, runs a couple of miles, becomes exhausted, and gives-up. Naturally, Tim would lose confidence in his ability to run the entire marathon and realizes that if he tried, he may injure himself. Putting himself to the test kept him honest about his abilities. But, more importantly, Tim's judgment improved as a result of making a realistic assessment of his own condition and what is possible in his performance. That informs him on where he needs to improve, and the amount of time and effort required to have satisfactory performance.

In another example, suppose Jill has never played golf, but thinks the game must be relatively simple. How difficult could it be, she wonders, to use the club to hit the ball into the hole? The first time she plays, she performs terribly and admits she underestimated game's difficulty. This type of failure is usually a letdown and may discourage some people from trying again. But by testing her ability and making measurable progress with practice, she can slowly increase the number of successful attempts. The more she repeats a successful attempt, the more she increases her confidence in her ability to do it again.

Testing can improve certainty in every part of the development process. If you remember a time when you studied for a test, and you quizzed yourself to see how many questions you could answer, you probably had some idea of how well you would do. If you answered all the questions correctly, you had a high level of confidence in your ability to pass the exam. This is sometimes called the testing effect.

Simply reading the material multiple times does not guarantee your ability to recall that material at a later time. But if you test your ability to recall the material as you read it, you can confirm that you are actually learning it.

To give another example, suppose John writes a speech and memorizes it. In his mind, he can imagine giving a great performance because he has completely memorized the speech. But as an amateur speaker who rarely gives public presentations, John has no idea how his performance will be delivered or received. So, when John gave his speech, he could remember it, but frequently stumbled in his presentation. He told a joke that, in his mind, was hilarious. But instead of hearing laughter, he heard silence and saw rolling eyes. These reactions gave John feedback on areas where he could improve.

Another way of quantifying performance is by calculating the rate of success or failure. A success-rate could be calculated by dividing the number of successful attempts by the total number of attempts. Zero percent indicates failure and would demonstrate a beginner, or introductory, level of ability. One-hundred percent would be a success and would demonstrate an expert, or advanced, level of ability. Each attempt could further be divided into a percentage. So, if your success rate at completing a task is .9 and your failure rate is .1, then you could focus on that additional 10 percent to reduce your failure rate and get over the learning curve. If all one-hundred percent of your attempts were completed without error, you should have absolute confidence in your success.

Testing can be especially useful in management roles. Each task an organization performs in the process of producing a product can be tested, measured, and improved.

And it's very difficult for management to have real confidence in organizational abilities without objective measures of performance and measuring the output of production. When management makes an intuitive guess about performance, that manager could be under-confident, which could lead to unnecessary stress, or over-confident, which could lead to failure.

Testing is also useful for training workers. Distributing information to workers hoping they will read it and apply it to their jobs, does not ensure that workers put those guidelines into practice. If management wants to ensure they do, they need to test workers and measure their success rate. It's better to test a worker's performance, and test the quality of that worker's production, to ensure that it meets sufficient quality standards. Workers who fail could be further trained in that specific area until the desired result is achieved. This way, management can gain a true sense of confidence, or lack thereof, in the organization's ability to perform as expected.

10
Critical Skills

Personal development is not always as easy or intuitive as people like to believe. It can require a considerable amount of effort in managing time constraints and overcoming difficult challenges. But it can also enable you to improve your overall condition and give you more control over your future. Skills development can improve your judgment and decision-making in specific roles, and increase your self-esteem and earnings potential. The only problem is, knowing the strength of your skills may require more than a subjective and intuitive belief.

If you need to develop a new skill, keep the Principle of Gradual Improvement in mind. Leverage time by creating a routine of gradually strengthening that skill with practice. To accelerate this progress, recognize and develop weak areas, especially those you are not able to perform, or that cause you to fumble and make mistakes.

If you are trying to change a habit, know that habits tend to be associated with environmental ques, and may also depend on skills and knowhow. The first part of developing a habit is to associate the correct response to environmental ques. For example, if you want to run five miles a day after you wake up, start by running half a mile. Doing that will associate the time of day with the act of running. After the habit is developed, then you can gradually increase or decrease the intensity as needed. If you want to be more effective in your exercise routine, look into methods for properly conditioning yourself and how to prepare healthy meals. Developing these additional skills can help you become more effective and successful in changing your habits. Without those skills, you are more likely to injure yourself, fail to follow through, and give-up.

Before you develop any skill, you should assess the amount of time required to develop that skill. Some skills can seem deceptively easy. For example, you can learn how to write a database application by following an online video. But writing enterprise application is a skill, comprised of many engineering skills with many learning curves, that requires years, and arguably a university degree, to fully develop.

Every skill has a different learning curve. Some are short and simple and can be developed in a matter of hours. Others can take years if not decades to master. So, you should ideally seek structured training to reduce the amount of time it takes to get over the learning curve, so you do not have to learn the hard way from trial-and-error or by learning from mistakes. That can consume a substantial amount of valuable time, and can become discouraging, and cause you to give-up. Training can help you identify weaknesses, avoid common mistakes, and provide you with techniques on getting over the learning curve faster.

One area where people often fail in their skills development is in having a realistic assessment, or expectation, of how confident they should be in their abilities. Under-confidence can cause you to avoid a challenge and give-up too easily. Over-confidence can cause you to not question the soundness of your judgment, and lead you to believe things that are untrue. Both under-confidence and over-confidence are subjective beliefs, not objective facts, and are more likely to cause mistakes and lead to failure.

To improve your assessment of your progress, and have a more accurate level of confidence in your abilities, base your assessment on objective and measurable results. If you base your progress on a subjective opinion (e.g., you worked hard, you are exhausted, and you now believe you have the right stuff), then you are more likely to fail. If you are in a competitive sport, you would have no way to compare how well your performance stacks-up against other athletes. Testing yourself and measuring your performance, especially in real-world scenarios, can give you better insight and feedback that can help you identify weak areas in your development that need more work.

PART IV:
ASSESSING MOTIVES

Understanding, and correctly interpreting, human motives, can have a strong influence on personal interactions, productivity, and cooperation. First and foremost, you have to be able to motivate yourself to achieve your own life goals. But also, knowing what drives people is an essential skill for being successful in many life roles, for example, if you are a parent, a manager, an organizational leader, an instructor, or in any other role where you have influence on other people's behavior, or development.

In the next chapter, we look at some basic theories of motivation, including my own theory of motivation that, I believe, does a better job at explaining human motives. It looks at why people value some things more than others, why people become emotional, and why people are motivated to seek fairness and justice. And in later chapters, we look at techniques for increasing personal productivity and techniques for strengthening cooperation and personal relationships.

CHAPTER 7:
A THEORY OF MOTIVATION

The ability to interpret and correctly judge human motives is, by itself, a basic personal skill required for maintaining healthy relationships. People who lack the ability to correctly interpret motives are more likely to misinterpret behavior or read too much into it, which can lead to misunderstandings and unnecessary conflict. Understanding motives also helps if you are trying to motivate people to perform at a higher level, for example of you are a leader trying to influence a team, a parent trying to influence a child, or an instructor trying to influence students.

In business, the inability to understand your customer's motives can increase or decrease demand for your product. Suppose management requires restaurant workers to upsell customers, meaning that if a customer orders a medium drink, the employee is required to ask if the customer wants a large drink for an additional 25 cents. But what if a worker automatically upgrades the order to a large without asking? Will customers be happier with a larger, more expensive item, than what they ordered? Or suppose a manager of a medical supplies company tries to reduce cost by using cheaper materials. Doing so enables the company to pass on the savings to their customers. But what if making those devices out of cheaper materials means producing an unsafe, defective, or substandard product? Will that increase sales? These two scenarios involve value creation, which is a subject we look at later in this chapter.

1

Theories of Motivation

During last few centuries, a number of competing theories about motivation have emerged from many different fields of study. And it helps to explore some of these theories, along with their strengths and weaknesses. Many of these arguably contain part-truths, or statements that are true some-of-the-time, but not all-of-the-time. Then we look at a more generalized theory of motivation.

One of the more popular theories in the business world is the Hierarchy of Needs published by Abraham Maslow, during the 1940's, in his paper entitled a *Theory of Human Motivation*. His theory suggests that when basic needs are met, like physiological needs, or the need for food and safety, a person can move on to higher needs for things like belonging and personal acceptance. This theory is useful for explaining social dynamics within families or at work. For example, when a person feels safe, that person may want to stay, bond, and form close relationships. But when a person feels threatened, or is isolated in the workplace and only see hostility, then one may be more resistant to forming relationships and may want to leave.

Another theory proposed by the Behaviorists, and Political and Economic theorists, is the idea that behavior is motivated by incentives, like rewards and punishments. This theory suggests that people are hedonistic and tend to be averse to pain and discomfort and avoid it, and prefer rewards and the pursuit of pleasure. Incentives, like financial gains, explains why people work hard to increase their income, seek social approval, and improve their standard of living. Incentives, like sanctions or punishments, also explains why people obey the law to avoid punishment.

But the problem with the universality of this theory is that people are not always motivated by incentives. First of all, people are constantly surrounded by things that could reward them with pleasure they do not pursue, whether it is food, relationships, or a lazy stroll in the park. During any time of the day, people could gamble, drink alcohol, or have sex. And businesses offer incentives to make purchases at discounts that buyers do not take advantage of. At any moment, a person could spend money on entertainment, but instead decides to work. And as people pursue their life interests, their goals may not even produce a financial reward, or the reward of happiness but, instead, may result in sacrifice and suffering. In fact, a person may risk one's life to help other people, which may never yield a reward but, instead, may be viewed as the right thing, the humane thing, or the moral thing to do.

Incentives can be effective for motivating behavior as we will see in this chapter, but not always. You cannot always bribe a person to commit any act, or punish a person into submission. If all behavior were motivated by incentives, you would never have to worry about an employee quitting a job so long as that worker's labor was sufficiently compensated. But people quit high-paying jobs for many reasons, because of stress that causes a decline in one's physical health, or because of poor relations, mismanagement, or other reasons. Rewards and punishments can provide short-term, immediate, results. But if you want to motivate people to be productive over a longer period of time, you need to combine incentives with other forms of motivation.

Another prominent theory of motivation is that people are motivated by goals. Human behavior, as we have seen throughout this book, is highly goal-oriented in that people are naturally driven to satisfy biological urges for nourishment, safety, and income. Research by Management and Organizational Psychologist Dr. Edwin Locke's *Goal Setting Theory of Motivation* suggests that when managers set clear and obtainable goals, worker productivity and performance increases. According to Dr. Locke, those goals should be slightly challenging to make the effort worth-while, but not so difficult that it leads to discouragement, giving-up, and failure. Goal setting is motivational because it defines a clear course of action and an end result to work toward so workers know where to focus their energy. When workers lack clear and obtainable goals, they are often less certain about what to do, more likely to be idle and unproductive, and more likely to fail.

Rational Choice Theory is a theory of motivation used in economic models, which suggests that people are motivated by their own self-interest and seek to increase their gains and cut their losses. When using this theory in economic models, a number of assumptions are made. First of all, the theory presumes that when people are rational actors, they make choices that benefit their self-interest and avoid choices that do not. So, given this assumption, we can predict the choice a rational buyer or seller would make in a given scenario, which tends to be the choice that yields the most financial gain or prevents the greatest loss. This can, then, be used to price goods and services, maximize profit, and determine whether a product is viable, based on whether enough demand exists in the market at a given price.

And lastly, the *Expectancy-Value Theory of Motivation*, developed by Jacquelynne Eccles, suggests that choices are motivated by 1) the expectation of success and 2) the subjective value of the task, or subjective task value. The first part suggests that if you do not expect to be successful, you have little motivation to try. And the second part suggests that people pursue things they want and value. Eccles further breaks down different types of value, like attainment value (i.e., the sense of accomplishment or achievement), the intrinsic value (i.e., the prospect of having an enjoyable experience), the utility value (i.e., the practicality or usefulness of the choice), and the cost value (i.e., what a person loses by making the choice, which may also include the opportunity to do other things).[51]

2
The Private Interest Theory of Motivation

The *Private Interest Theory of Motivation* suggests that people are motivated by private interests, which sounds like Rational Choice Theory, except we make no assumption about a person's interests. Private, in the term private interests, refers to the idea that motives are abstract and cannot always be observed or known, sometimes even to the person who has them. This is different from shared interests, which are private interests that people share among one another. For example, marriage partners both have an interest in marriage. When lawmakers draft laws, they are operating in the public interest, which is a type of shared interest among community members. All people want roads and bridges to commute on (i.e., shared interests) so they can obtain the things they want (i.e., private interests).

Motivation requires a combination of both interest and expectations. Interests always drive behavior because people attend to what they are interested in the moment. *Interest*, itself, is the ability to see value, or potential value, in something, like learning, exploring, participating in an activity, or going to an event. People often see value in things that provide a benefit, even if it's only an emotional benefit. For example, eating candy or watching television may not have much practical or monetary value. But people see value in those activities because they provide enjoyment or relaxation.

Expectations about the value of things, and your ability to obtain them, also influences your motivation. In fact, expectations about value can influence interest. An expectation of low value, can make you disinterested. An expectation of high value can motivate a person to want it, and try to obtain it. Even if something has high value but you cannot obtain it, then you have little motivation to try.

To illustrate the idea of how interests and expectations motivate behavior, imagine you are on an expedition for lost treasure. The treasure, in this example, is pure potential value. You have no idea whether you will find the treasure, despite risking your life. But you are motivated, not only by an expectation of finding a valuable cache of treasure, but to seek out information or experiences that could confirm or change your expectations. As you intuitively interact with, and speculate about, the world around you, you are attempting to follow the value where it leads you, which sometimes leads to dead-ends.

As people interact with their environment, they have immediate interests within the context of their immediate circumstances. And those interests tend to drive their attention and cognitive focus more than anything else. At any moment, a person may want to satisfy a biological urge, like eating or using the rest room. These interests tend to drive purchasing decisions, productivity, political affiliation, and even criminal acts. People obey laws, strive to earn their income, and protect and defend their family, career, and causes, because by doing so, they obtain more of what they want. At the same time, people commit crimes, knowingly victimize and harm other people, to gain more of what they want. Of course, these two approaches can also have very different consequences that people may, or may not, want to live with.

Human values and wants drive human productivity and the development of new capabilities far more than basic existential needs. To illustrate why, imagine a scenario in which you are stranded on a deserted island. You can satisfy your basic needs for nourishment by eating slimy worms and living in a flimsy shelter made of tree branches. But in the back of your mind, you would always want something more satisfying, like a fish cooked over an open flame, or a three-course meal at a fancy restaurant. And you may be willing to sacrifice a little more energy and effort to obtain those things. As the Rational Choice Theory suggests, people want the better, more desirable, option among alternatives. And those human wants, rather than the most basic existential needs, are the driving force that has propelled the human civilization from the stone-age into the world of science and technology, and toward ever-increasing loftier goals for a better quality of life and a better standard of living.

The pursuit of private interest can drive people to be both more selfless or more selfish. It makes people more selfless when they want to cooperate with others in the pursuit of shared interests, for example, in starting a friendship, business partnership, or family. If you are interested in making the world better in some way, you may want to join an organization that will help to do that. But private interest also makes people more selfish as they are motivated to protect and defend their interests. People can isolate themselves, avoid cooperating with others, or create unnecessary conflicts, to protect what they have. And that is especially true in communities were members distrust one another over fears about crime or social problems.

3

Value Creation

An important question in Economics and in the Human Sciences is: Why do people value some things more than others? And how is value created? The first question may have already been answered in an earlier chapter when we looked at how people, early in their lives, develop an inclination to favor some things over others. Those inclinations become your preferences, wants, and values. Many of those inclinations become your personal and cultural values, which include personal qualities, family traditions, cultural beliefs, or hobbies. And those values can influence what you value in the marketplace.

Economic value is the price that buyers are willing to pay for goods and services in the marketplace. *Market value*, in Economics, is the price determined by the seller, who typically wants the highest price compared to similar items in the market. But ultimately, the buyer's decision to purchase the item, depends on how much that person wants the item at that price. And the buyer may not want the item, for a number of reasons. Other sellers in the market may be selling it at a lower price. Or the stated price may be more than what the buyer wants to pay. In some circumstances, the seller may be willing to negotiate on the price, depending on how much the seller wants to sell the item.

Economic models that analyze price fluctuations in the marketplace can involve many complex factors. But we can also use a crude supply and demand model to understand what drives value in the marketplace. In the simplest supply and demand model, when the supply of an item is high and the demand is low, the price of the item tends to be low. This would be similar to an item a seller has too much of, and has difficulty getting rid of, because buyers can find the same item at a lower price elsewhere. This can happen after holidays when buyers have already done their holiday shopping. So, merchants put holiday decorations on the clearance isle at deeply discounted prices. In contrast, when the supply of an item is low and the demand is high, the price of an item tends to be high. This would be similar to a rare one-of-a-kind painting coming up for sale by a very popular artist. Anytime you have a desirable item in low supply, and lots of buyers, the price of that item tends to go up.

So, the monetary exchange value of an item depends on how much people demand, or want, that item at its current supply. People value an item based on whether they want it enough to give-up their hard-earned money to obtain it. The more a person wants an item, the greater amount of time, money, or labor, the buyer may be willing to sacrifice, in payment, for the item.

What this means is that if you can create something people want, whether it is a tangible object or knowhow, you can create value. In business, that may mean creating a new product, or innovating an existing product. For example, you could by an old piece of furniture and restore it, and a buyer may be willing to pay a higher price for it. The value to the buyer comes from not having to waste one's valuable time and energy doing that work but, instead, paying someone else to do it. This added value is also called a *value driver*, which is something that adds value to an option and makes it more attractive than the alternative. When faced with more than one option, the tendency to choose the one with greater perceived value, follows Rational Choice Theory.

When knowledge and skills have monetary exchange value, they are sometimes called human capital. The price of labor increases for many reasons, for example, when a position requires a high level of expertise, when a shortage of labor exists in the market, or when trained professionals provide a superior quality of work. But skilled labor is also valuable because it decreases unnecessary costs. Without the required skills, management is helpless to do anything about many business-related problems, like software development, accounting, or legal representation. To resolve those problems, management is forced to pay an outside contractor, who may not have the best interests of the company in mind, to perform the same work. So, management needs to determine whether it is more advantageous to hire a skilled worker, or pay an outside business the perform the same work. If management is incapable of getting the right mix of skilled talent, the business will suffer.

People do not always consider market prices when making value-based decisions. They can value things more or less, depending on their own private interests. For example, a person may value certain material artifacts, like family heirlooms, folk items, or memorabilia, above or below market prices depending on their private interests. And researchers have found that people tend to value their own possessions and ideas more than other people's, which is sometimes called the endowment effect. The over-valuing of one's own ideas and possessions above other peoples', can cause the seller to over-price items that one wants to keep.

4
The Effect of Gains & Losses

As people pursue their private interests, they tend to be drawn toward things they want to gain, like improving their social status or increasing their financial wealth, and avoid things they do not want, like losing money or endangering their physical safety. This could also be called the Effect of Gains and Losses, or the Gain/Loss Theory of Motivation. To make a calculated decision, you may want to consider what you stand to gain or lose because it could have positive or negative repercussions for your physical or financial condition.

Productivity is highly motivated by the prospect of gains or the threat of losses. On a biological level, people are motivated to pursue opportunities to make wanted gains, in terms of security, nourishment, help, or anything that leads to growth and development. That means protecting oneself from the threat of losses, like the loss of food, safety, help, or any resource that could result in physical decline, weakness, loss of employment, or death. Similarly, productivity is motivated by the prospect of financial gains in the labor market, or the threat of future losses as a result of not maintaining possessions or not being prepared for the future.

In many ways, this idea is similar to an incentive-based theory of motivation. If gains are rewarding and losses are punishing, then people may be motivated to make future gains and avoid future losses. Since people are motivated by their own interests, rather than arbitrary incentives, things that are of particular interest to them, like money or freedom, tend to incentivize their behavior. This is why wanted behaviors, like talent in the labor market, are rewarded with financial gains, and why unwanted behaviors, like violating legal prohibitions, are punished with losses, like fines or jail time.

Part of the reason losses are effective in deterring or punishing prohibited behavior among most people is that they gain, what some Economists call, a Penalty Avoidance Benefit, which is the benefit a person or business receives from operating in accordance with laws and regulations.[48] Many of those benefits include keeping your money, freedom, additional liberties, additional protections, and certain advantages in the marketplace where a criminal record would put you at a disadvantage. So, people are motivated to avoid legal infractions that make them more susceptible to avoidable fines, prosecution, and incarceration, and other forms of losses, like being subject to greater intolerance and discrimination, depending on the nature of the crime.

But the prospect of gains or losses can also incentivize people to behave dishonestly. Anytime a person is threatened by a loss of income, employment, companionship, or social acceptance, that loss can incentivize that person to lie, and behave dishonestly, to avoid losing those things. In the workplace, a worker may lie about one's credentials or expertise to gain promotional opportunities, or lie about one's shortcomings or mistakes to protect one's employment from accusations of wrongdoing.

The quality of a decision is strongly associated with whether it produces a gain or a loss. And when a decision results in a wanted gain or a wanted loss, that decision tends to be judged as a good or rational decision. In fact, during my time in business school, students were taught that good decisions are those that make both the buyer and seller better off. In this win-win scenario, the buyer gets the desired good or service and the seller gets the desired compensation. So, when both get what they want, they agree it was a good decision. But when a person gains at the expense of others, or causes a person to experience an unfair loss, like a crime of theft, that tends to be viewed as an act of injustice.

What people consider to be a gain or loss is also relative to their private interests. The problem with incentives, alone, is that losing an unwanted thing is not necessarily perceived as a loss or a punishment. And gaining unwanted thing is not necessarily perceived as a gain or a reward. In fact, people endure punishment and forgo rewards to gain, or avoid losing, something they really want. So, people not only judge the quality of decisions based on whether they result in gains or losses, but based on whether those results are in their best interests. If Jim is seeking spiritual enlightenment and forgoes financial opportunities to obtain that enlightenment, in his mind, he is making the best decision for him. But Sara, who is desperately seeking more financial opportunities, thinks that Jim is making an unwise decision. So, Sara does not trust Jim's judgment. Whether a decision is perceived to be good and rational is completely relative to that person's unique interests, ambitions, and life goals.

Psychologists Daniel Kahneman and Amos Tversky, famed for their research on human judgment, did studies on how gains or losses influence behavior. According to their research, people tend to be loss averse and avoid losses, more than they pursue gains. If we look at the big-picture view of why that is, people are cautious and want to avoid losing the little they have. And usually, some type of risk (i.e., the risk of losses) is involved with making gains. For example, quitting your job to pursue a higher paying job. Or taking out debt to finance education. If you are uncertain about whether a decision will result in a wanted gain or an unwanted loss, you may avoid it all together to avoid the loss. After all, you cannot be certain about what you stand to gain, but you can be absolutely certain about what you stand to lose. So, you protect yourself by proceeding with caution, to avoid costly mistakes.

The problem with completely avoiding unwanted losses is that gaining more of what you want requires the expenditure of time, money, and opportunities. Those losses are not the result of poor decisions. Instead, they are necessary to gain more of what you want. That would be, what an Economist would call, a sunk cost, which is a loss that you are not able to get back and should not regret. Another problem is that while people may be constantly striving to make the best choices for themselves, they sometimes make undesirable choices that cannot be avoided. This is because people have limited means and are forced to accept trade-offs. Since people have limitations in time and finances, they are forced to make a choice, and forgo the opportunity to do something else, which may not be the best choice.

5

Emotional Consequences

The effect of gains and losses not only influences decision-making, it also has a tremendous effect on a person's emotional state of mind. You can observe this when a person wins a game, receives social approval, lands a new job, or gets married. All of these evoke joy and happiness. Losses, on the other hand, like losing a game, social disapproval, employment termination, or having something stolen from you, can evoke anger or sadness, or hurtful feelings.

In terms of lower, instinctual, abilities, people have warning systems (e.g., fear), or biological defenses (e.g., anger), that serve to protect them from losses to their physical safety, personal relationships, or financial status. Usually these systems are helpful, like when fear protects you from losing life and limb in a horrible accident. Or when stress levels increase while trying to complete a project on time. But other times, fear can override reason and cause people to behave irrationally. For example, when a motorist is late for work and is losing time, that motorist may drive at unsafe speeds, putting oneself and other motorists at risk.

Even the smallest gains or losses, like losing an argument or winning a bet, can influence a person's happiness. A few years ago, a colleague of mine began celebrating because he was winning a video game on his mobile phone. His winnings had no practical use or monetary value. But he was ecstatic and celebrating because he was a winner. This same excitement occurs among fans at sports events. The fans of the winning team celebrate in victory, while the fans of the losing team are shocked, horrified, and emotionally crushed as they watch their team's defeat. At the Euro 2016 Championship, rivalry between Russian and English football fans was so intense and so emotionally charged that police resorted to firing tear gas into the crowds, and made arrests, to stop fans from fighting in the streets.[58]

Research has found that a person's financial status may have some positive or negative effect on a person's overall sense of happiness, or life satisfaction. According to a Pew

Research Center survey, people with more education, income, and household goods, experienced greater satisfaction than people without those things. The survey looked at whether the participants had specific household goods, like a "television, refrigerator, washing machine, microwave oven, computer, car, bicycle, motorcycle/scooter and radio." Many of these, like the car or washing machine, are conveniences that reduce the burden and workload of living, which enables people to spend more time enjoying life. The greater number of items the participants possessed, the greater amount of happiness they reported experiencing. But the participants also said that some things were more important than financial prosperity, like "health, their children's education and being safe from crime."[44]

The pursuit of financial wealth can also cause unnecessary distress. When people work longer hours, and more of their time, labor, and attention is demanded by clients or employers, it increases unhealthy stress levels and can lead to unhealthy lifestyle habits. Married couples who place a high value on financial gains may start arguments and conflicts over financial concerns and potential financial losses. They may blame each other, or harbor resentment, for financial losses. And those feelings can lead to more conflicts that increase stress levels and put a strain on the relationship.

According to researchers Ryan Howell at San Francisco State University and Thomas Gilovich at Cornell University, people are happier when they spend their money on experiences that make them happy, like playing games or going to sports events, rather than tangible objects. The happiness gained from possessing a material item fades over time, while the happiness from an experience may be recalled and shared numerous times. Happy experiences also tend to include family and friends, and can be shared with other people in conversations or social media. Gilovich suggested that to improve the happiness of citizens, policy makers should consider creating more public works projects designed to provide citizens with opportunities for positive experiences in the community.[30]

Political and economic circumstances can cause people to experience unfair losses and drive discontent and unhappiness in communities. For example, citizens may experience losses to their health and safety as a result of urban decay, the rise in crime, or unfair discrimination. People who face unfair discrimination, for example, experience unfair losses in the form of lost job opportunities, income, and other types of opportunities. And that can be hurtful emotionally and financially, and can prevent people from generating wealth, starting businesses, or introducing new ideas. That lack of opportunity leaves the community poorer, less contented, and less happy. That's why creating and enforcing policies that protect citizens and prevent unfair discrimination makes communities wealthier, more capable of solving its problems, and generally happier.

6

Inequity

In life, you will experience unfairness or injustice that could be generally called inequity. All people experience unfairness as you will experience unequal treatment or unequal advantage. This is something that you probably discovered at an early age when treated differently by caregivers, or when your peers were give more privileges. But when that unfairness causes significant harm, it can become an injustice. And justice, by contrast, can be thought of as rectifying an unfair situation that caused significant harm or loss.

People have expectations about personal treatment, and what they gain or give up, in their personal relationships. Anytime someone experiences an unexpected loss as a result of another person's actions, that could be considered unfair. The economic definition of a fair exchange is one in which both parties agree to the terms of the exchange. So, if one person gains at the expense of the other, and the person on the losing side did not agree to the loss, that would be unfair. Just like if you paid for a product that you did not receive, you would consider that unfair. This is one of the reasons people write agreements and sign contracts, to protect themselves from unacceptable losses they did not expect or agree to.

When a person experiences a significant and unexpected loss as a result of another person's actions, like the loss of property, the loss of health and safety, or the loss of a loved one, people tend to view that action as unfair. And if that unfair loss is never paid back or compensated, it becomes an injustice. Since people do not want to continue to experiencing injustice, they may be motivated to prevent the perpetrator from repeating the offense by taking action against the offender. Historically, these types of actions have created long-standing feuds and wars between families, neighbors, and larger groups of people, as they become locked in an exchange of retaliation crimes. The criminal justice system provides public services to deter and rectify injustices with law enforcement and civil services to prevent revenge or retaliation crimes and maintain civil order.

Already we have seen how inequity can motivate a desire to restore justice. But does inequity also motivate criminal behavior. Research has found that income inequality may be one of the motiving factors of criminal behavior. In 1968, Economist Gary Becker speculated that criminals may do a short-hand version of cost-benefit analysis in which they weigh the odds of getting caught with the potential payoff. Some research suggests that communities with greater income disparities are more likely to have higher violent crime rates. Robert Merton developed "strain theory," which suggests that crime occurs because people are under social pressure to achieve socially accepted goals, but lack the means. And the strain of the social pressure motivates people to commit crimes.[46]

Adversity may also play a role in crime. People face adversity for many reasons during their youth, because of harsh treatment from parents of piers, or as a result of living in poverty. And adversity can be very isolating. A person who does not feel cared about, or feels hurt, by others may reciprocate those feelings. When a person has negative experiences when interacting with others frequently enough, those feelings can become generalized and projected onto complete strangers. And that deranged thinking can create reasons to commit crimes, like theft or a mass-shooting. As a side-note, a law enforcement officer in my city stated that many of their arrests are due to substance use or addictions.

Social injustice occurs when people are treated differently or denied opportunities because of race, ethnicity, sex, or other factors. And that can have a significant impact on people affected by those injustices, as a result of losing freedoms, opportunities, and personal safety. Economic injustice occurs when people who live in poorer communities and lack the same opportunities as people who live in wealthier communities. To illustrate this idea, imagine two communities that coexist, side-by-side. On one side of the street, people have access to safe food and drinking water, functional infrastructure, protection from crime and environmental hazards, and access to job opportunities and income. And on the other side of the street, people do not have access to healthy food or clean water, access to transportation, employment opportunities, business opportunities, or equal protection under the law.

When citizens of a community have greater protection from these forms of injustice, they experience fewer instances of unfairness, fewer reasons to be discontented, and greater satisfaction within the community. When policy makers do a better job at prohibiting or rectifying social and economic injustice, it not only reduces the discontent created by those injustices, more people have opportunities to generate wealth, contribute ideas to solve problems, and people tend to be happier and more contented as a result of experiencing fewer instances of unfairness, conflict, and unnecessary strife in the community.

7

Critical Skills

Knowing how to interpret human motives is a basic skill that can reduce misunderstandings, conflict, and improve personal relationships. You cannot always correctly judge a person's motives based on one's actions. And decisions that result in negative consequences are not always motivated by malicious intent, but may be a simple mistake or a misunderstanding.

Motives are also highly influenced by private interests. Knowing this, by itself, can help you motivate other people by attempting to drive interest in what you are doing. But it also helps you to avoid misunderstandings. As people go about their business, they act in their own interests. And that, by itself, can be mistaken for behaving selfishly, especially when someone, or something, is ignored that would benefit other people.

While people often compare themselves to other people, judging others, or their decisions, based on your values may not fair to them since your values differ from theirs. It's easy to look at another person's decisions as odd in the context of you own interests and values and conclude that you would never make that decision. That, of course, does not mean the other person is less intelligent. It simply means that person has different interests, different values, and different life pursuits.

You can also create value by creating something that people want, whether it is a skill or service, creating a new product, or work that improves an existing product. From an individual perspective, doing this can increase your own self-esteem and your earnings potential. But from a business perspective, understanding this can be useful when trying to retain and increase customers. If a business puts a policy or process in place that serves the business's interests, but leaves their customers less satisfied, the business may see a decline.

The gains and losses people experience, especially when it concerns their private interests and obtaining the things they want, can significantly affect them, even on an emotional level. That's why the prospect of making gains, or avoiding losses, is such a significant driver of productivity and personal development. But it can also motivate people to seek justice when they experience unfair losses, like when someone gains at their expense.

In business, when a customer buys a service, but receives far less than what was expected, it can influence the buyer's decision about whether to continue doing business with the service provider. If the perceived unfairness, or loss, is great enough, it could motivate someone to seek justice, or prevent the offender from doing it again, with the help of legal services. So, if you are trying to motivate consumers to buy a product, or motivate employees to stay with the business, then creating a since of fairness is one way of bringing about that end result. Business owners could further create policies that prohibit unfair treatment, and make an effort to enforce those prohibitions, to prevent discontent and dissatisfaction that could motivate further personal attacks or resignations.

CHAPTER 8:
MOTIVATING PRODUCTIVITY

People often fail to achieve their goals because they are not productive enough. And if you are striving to achieve some personal or organizational goal, you need to learn how to motivate yourself or other people to be more productive. Doing that can be particularly useful in roles where you are required to motivate people, if you are a leader, parent, instructor, manager, and so on.

In this chapter, we look at a number of techniques for motivating productivity. One of the oldest ways is by threat or coercion. This is often the tool of powerful people who use the power of the State to threaten people's lives to get what they want. While that can motivate productivity in the short-term, as a person tries to avoid the negative consequences, it can also backfire if it motivates that person to retreat, escape, or fight back, out of their innate natural desire for safety and protection. So, in this chapter, we look at a variety of other, and arguably more ethical, techniques for motivating productivity by appealing to people's private interests, to help them understand why being more productive is in their best interests.

1
Productivity

In Economics, *productivity* is a measure of the amount of work performed, and specifically a measure of output, in terms of the amount of product (i.e., goods and services produced). Productivity, in your own life, may be measured by the amount of time and energy spent working towards achieving a goal. If you want to continue to make progress toward creating a more satisfying life, instead of squandering and wasting your opportunities, you need to stay productive. The more you accomplish now, and the greater number of goals you achieve right-away, the more satisfied you will be with your life.

Human effort is one of the most influential factors that determines success beyond the planning phase. Without enough effort, projects fail. As you work towards achieving your goals, you will face difficulties and make mistakes. Making an effort successful usually does not hinge upon any single pivotal decision, but instead a series of decisions, a sustained effort, and a hard-fought march toward a desired end. During that process, you will make many mistakes, and experience significant gains and losses. And those difficulties can be overwhelming and discouraging at times. As you learn from mistakes and get better with practice, you can discover new approaches that will help you to be more successful the next time.

2
Cognitive Focus

Your productivity largely depends on your cognitive focus, which includes your ability stay on task, read and learn, and have the stick-to-it-iveness to follow through with personal goals. Without a strong cognitive focus, it becomes difficult to complete even simple goals. So, the more you can focus on your work, unobstructed by distractions, the more work you can complete in a shorter period of time.

Immediate interests, and what people attend to in the moment, is a common reason people lose their cognitive focus. Those immediate interests may include responding to biological urges (i.e., bathroom breaks, meals, or discomfort), or responding to life circumstances. When immediate interests drive behavior more than far distant future outcomes, researchers sometimes call that temporal discounting, or time discounting. In other words, what is happening now is far more important than what will happen in the future.

To illustrate this idea, imagine that Adam has a goal to exercise and eat healthy. At the moment, he is sitting on the couch, eating potato chips, and watching television, which is far more relaxing than getting physical exercise. He always has time to exercise and eat healthy in the future. So, he might as well enjoy this moment while it lasts, even if it lasts until tomorrow, the next day, and into perpetuity. While people, like Adam, have the ability to think strategically and consider long-term consequences, they can also be easily distracted by current events, current needs that have to be met, and promises that have to be kept, which can cause people to lose focus on longer-term goals. For many people, this may be the perfect excuse for not scheduling more time to be productive.

3
Goal Setting

Goal setting is one of the best ways to improve motivation and productivity. One truth about human behavior that is repeated frequently throughout this book is that behavior and its motives are highly goal oriented. At a biological level, you are motivated to pursue goals for satiation, safety, self-protection, and excretion, all of which are necessary for survival. You also have complex human goals that require the ability to recognize, and make predictions about, future outcomes. Those social goals tend to be more complex and require thinking, planning, and strategy, and may depend on the development of intellectual abilities or personal relationships.

According to Dr. Edwin Locke's Goal-Setting Theory of behavior, goalsetting is effective in driving productivity because it provides you with a well-defined course of action. Without clear goals or a clear plan of action, it's difficult to know how to proceed, and what activities to engage in. In fact, people who lack clear goals can become directionless, and may not know what to do. You could take your life in the wrong direction or spend your time idly doing nothing, only to regret it later. Teenagers and young adults often spend a great deal of time on activities that do not necessarily make their lives better because they have not yet established clearly defined life goals that they are working toward. Without goalsetting, you are more likely to lose cognitive focus, forget about your goals, and pursue your immediate interests.

To be successful at achieving your goals, you need to consider the complexity of the goal and the amount of time available in your schedule to work toward achieving that goal. If you set the bar low and pursue easy challenges, you can have a high level of success at anything you try. But if the bar is too high, like trying to fit the Universe into a mathematical equation, you will struggle to be successful at anything. Similarly, you may be hesitant to start working on big insurmountable goals. But you can also leverage time and break down large complex goals into smaller, more manageable, goals. Setting easier goals for yourself increases your ability to be successful. And as you make progress, you build a track-records of success, and build confidence in your ability to be successful.

Your productivity tends to correspond with the number of goals you achieve. So, if you want to increase your motivation, or that of other people, you need to set more goals that will help you to schedule your time and know where to focus your energy. To define your goals, try to identify problems that could lead to dissatisfaction, or what is missing from your life, which could be a relationship, income, or something else.

4
Time Management

To be successful in achieving your life goals, you have to allocate enough time on your schedule to pursue the things you want. This is basic arithmetic. The following time management strategies can help you to increase the amount of time you have to work toward achieving your goals.

First, start with low-hanging fruit. Complete small, manageable, tasks that can be done right-way, especially those that need to be done. If you are working on a project that has a due date, get more work done sooner (e.g., preliminary brainstorming, research, and rough draft) to give yourself more time to improve the quality of the work and reduce stress about the pending deadline. When you are able to accomplish more earlier, you create a time surplus, which gives you more time in the future to improve the quality of your work and pursue the things you want.

Prioritize goals that are most important to you. As you grow older, you will accumulate more things you want to do. But as you put more goals into your future, you accumulate more time deficits. Instead of getting ahead, you always find yourself falling behind. So, decide which goals you want to achieve now, and which goals can wait until later.

Create a realistic and doable schedule. You may be ambitious and create a long daily to-do list. But attempting to do everything at a breakneck speed is not the wisest time management strategy because it can lead to stress, mistakes, accidents, and poor decisions. You need to understand the amount of time a task will take. If you do not know how much time a task will take, try performing the task once or twice, and then create a schedule based on those estimates. You should also give yourself plenty of time to do high priority tasks. If your employer expects you to be at work at a specific time, give yourself plenty of time so you are not angry at slow drivers, stressed out, and late to work.

Have patience as you work toward your goal. People like to demand immediate results and, because of that, sometimes create unrealistic goals. If you want to body-build and have never trained before, then starting with heaviest weights would be an unrealistic expectation that could put you in the hospital. A more effective approach would be to start with smaller goals, like lifting smaller weights in sets of repetitions, and then slowly working up to heavier weights after you have developed the muscles to do so.

Assess your condition realistically and know your core competencies. If you expect to be an expert in a subject within a matter of months, but have never made an attempt to learn anything about that subject, your expectations may be unrealistic. If you are completely new to computer programming, you may be able to learn the syntax of the language relatively quickly, but it may take months or years to learn more advanced topics that a more experienced programmers can learn in hours, days, or weeks. For example, a person who did programming for the last thirty years can learn a new language quicker than a beginner, especially if it's similar to other languages that person has used. So, you can achieve success quicker, and reduce your time and energy investment, if you build on strengths and core competencies you already possess.

Leverage time by breaking-down large time-consuming tasks into smaller, more manageable, tasks that are more likely to pay off. If you have a large project, like building a computer desk, break it down into more manageable parts. One day your goal may be to work out the design and decide on its appearance and construction techniques. The next day you could take measurements and decide on the wood. The next day you could purchase the wood. And the next day you could cut the wood, and so on. Making progress in small increments, like a few hours a day or a few hours on the weekend, is better than making no progress at all. Eventually, your desk will be built and hopefully you will be satisfied with the result.

And lastly, avoid overworking yourself. People logically assume that if they do not work hard enough right-away, they will fail. But productivity also puts stress and strain on the brain and body. Rest and sleep enable your brain and body to recover from work by replenishing nutrients to organs that could be damaged by nutrient deficiencies, enabling your body's systems to operate normally. Sleep deprivation can cause fatigue and exhaustion, and can impair the brain's ability to function. Excessive stress or a loss of sleep can cause a decline in your ability to learn, pay attention, and use good judgment. So, getting enough rest and sleep can improve how well your mental systems operate, which improves your decision-making and strengthens your overall condition.

5
Creativity

As you productively work toward your goals, you may need to be creative, and use your imagination to create work that evokes the right emotion. This is not only true if you need to be creative in your profession, if you are an artist of some type, but in your private life as well. For example, if you want to remodel your living space, or host a dinner that you want to be entertaining. Or if you are an instructor, you may have to think creatively about how to teach a difficult topic. So, knowing techniques for being more creative can instrumental in helping you to be productive.

One technique for being more creative involves envisioning what is missing in a picture or arrangement and trying to fill-in that void. Gestalt psychology shows us that the human brain does this automatically. Your brain is incapable of accurately perceiving all of the minor and insignificant details in the world around you. So, it automatically fills-in missing details of your perception to create a more organized, meaningful, and complete mindscape of reality.

People also do this in their deliberate thinking, when

they draw from the palette of their interests to envision and create the lives they want. The incompleteness we perceive in our lives, which sometimes leaves us dissatisfied, can trigger our creative-urge to fill-in that void, just as an appetite needs to be nourished, or a mystery needs to be revealed, or a problem needs to be solved, or a goal needs to be achieved.

Discovery is another important part of the creative process. Sometimes that may involve discovering what you have to work with by playing with the materials, adding to them, subtracting from them, changing them, replacing them, or recombining them in new patterns. Creativity sometimes occurs by fusing two ideas together to make something new. But experimentation alone cannot guarantee that you, or anyone else, will be satisfied with the end result. So, when trying to make new discoveries, you may want to draw inspiration from projects that have proven themselves to be successful.

Discoveries can also be made by looking at another person's work, especially work that sparks your interest, as an example of how to solve a similar problem. If you want to remodel your living space, look at existing examples for ideas, and tailor those ideas to fit your needs by adding to them or innovating them. You could seek education so you do not have to learn the hard-way using trial-and-error experimentation. When you are forced to learn from your mistakes, it consumes an enormous amount of time, and you more likely to fail and give-up. As you acquire more experience, and learn different techniques for solving the same problems, you accumulate a repository of knowledge of what works. Alternatively, if you want something that is more impressive, that is beyond your capabilities, consider hiring someone who has that expertise and can bring good ideas to the table.

And lastly, model your idea on paper before investing a substantial amount of time and money into building it. Planning your idea on paper can help you to study, analyze, and improve your design. Documentation can also help you share and receive feedback on your idea, understand project requirements, discover problems beforehand, determine the project's viability and budget, and create a realistic time-line for project completion, long before you make regretta-ble mistakes.

6

Motivating Others

At some point in life, you may find yourself in a role where you need to influence people's behavior to achieve a desired end. That is certainly true if you are an organizational leader, instructor, coach, or in some other role, in which mo-tivating behavior can influence an outcome. Interestingly, one of the goals of marketing is to motivate people to buy products. And marketers have some interesting strategies that could help us understand how to motivate people more effectively.

First of all, know your target audience and, specifically, know what their interests are. If you are a business owner trying to increase sales, marketing your product to the wrong people is not going to help. You need to establish who your audience is and why they are interested in what you are selling. Marketers sometimes do this by dividing populations into demographic segments, by grouping peo-ple together based on similar interests. For example, young people are more likely to attend rock concerts, or new parents are more likely to need diapers. Trying to sell something to someone who is not interested is like putting money in a pile and burning it.

Controlling attention is another way marketers gain influence over buyer decisions. The whole purpose of advertisement is to divert people's attention away from what they are doing to show them why they want a product. If you can control attention without annoying or harassing people, you may convince people that buying your product is in their best interests. But if you are not able to control attention, your target audience will not know anything about your product.

Changing expectations is also essential for changing the choices people make. Anytime people see a new idea, a new product, or a new restaurant, they may not know what to expect. If a friend tells you that a Restaurant's food is terrible and gave them food poisoning, does it influence your expectations about the Restaurant and your decision to dine there? Of course, it may have some influence. The things people expect to gain from what they give-up in time and money, has a tremendous influence on their choices. People usually do not take out large sums of debt to finance an expensive education if they do not expect to increase their income and pay back the debt. Those expectations influence a person's life choices, productivity, behavior, and personal sacrifices.

Sales and marketing people spend much of their careers trying to influence buyer expectations by showing buyers how a product makes life better, more entertaining, improves health, or sex appeal. Even how a product makes a person feel can influence their expectations. So, marketers sometimes use a technique called emotional branding. For instance, a car commercial may show a woman who cannot contain her excitement about her new car, its warranty, and how it drives. This not only associates the brand with positive feelings, but viewers of the commercial will want the same experience. Or a restaurant commercial will show people dining at their restaurant who are laughing and enjoying the food to make viewers of the commercial want the same experience.

Brand reputation can also have a tremendous influence on buyer choices. Earlier in this book, we briefly look at research by Psychologists Amos Tversky and Daniel Kahneman, which suggested that people tend to be loss averse, and are cautious about the choices they make. If you do not know anything about a product, it puts you at greater risk of an unwanted purchase. So, you may choose a brand you are already familiar with and have some confidence in. This is a substantial barrier to entry for many new products, and is why new businesses have to develop a strong differentiation strategy to show how their product is different, or better, than their competitors.

7
Incentive-Based Motivation

In the previous section, we looked at how people respond to incentives as a result of what they expect to gain or lose. Political and Economic theorists have long touted incentives as a way of influencing behavior. After all, those incentives are why people perform work in exchange for payment, or avoid legal prohibitions to avoid fines. But how effective are incentives on changing behavior?

In his book *Drive: The Surprising Truth About What Motivates Us*, Daniel Pink cites numerous examples of how people tend to be motivated by intrinsic rewards, and the desire to do something, rather than extrinsic rewards and punishments, like money or the threat of imprisonment, as the Rational Choice Theory suggests.[45] According to Pink, people do not always have to be compensated to perform work, which may explain why some software developers regularly make contributions to Open-Source projects without any expectation of monetary compensation.

One reason Open-Source projects are successful is not that people like to slavishly work for free, but because they have some intrinsic value to gain from it. People like to volunteer their time and labor to worthy causes where it is needed. And that gives them an opportunity to apply and develop their skills, demonstrate their talent, or gain valuable experience. That intrinsic motivation, Pink says, has contributed to the rise of Wikipedia and the decline of traditional for-profit encyclopedias.

Pink cites a number of studies that show how increasing incentives, like monetary compensation, does not always increase the quality or quantity of work. In some instances, the quality actually decreases, like when a person takes shortcuts to achieve a goal, or when a person is corrupted by the anticipation of increasing rewards. If management offers a bonus for filling a sales quota, sales associates may do whatever is necessary, including lying to potential buyers, to make sales. Many fast-food businesses incentivize their employees to upsell customers so that when you buy a meal, they offer you a larger drink or the more expensive item. If the order taker simply charges the customer for the more expensive item, which has happened to me on a number of occasions, that transaction may not leave the customer happy and wanting to come back.

Another problem with providing external, monetary, incentives for specific behaviors is that people tend to stop performing work when the reward is no longer provided. If a parent pays a child to perform a chore, like taking out the garbage, and the parent fails to pay one week, the child may stop performing the chore. People are motivated by rewards and punishments, Pink argues, but they are motivated by much more than the incentives proposed by Rational Choice Theory.

This intrinsic motivation that Pink wrote about is unmistakably the pursuit of private interest. If a child stops taking out the garbage due to a lack of payment, it's because the compensation itself became the goal, rather than maintaining a clean home. Passion drives productivity and quality. But without interest, passion does not exist. People need to have interest, and see some value in doing something, before they will voluntarily do it. This is why so many fully capable grade-school students fail. The extrinsic motivators of grades or scholarship are not enough to make them interested in the curriculum. If they were, they would voluntarily do it without being told, similar to a health-conscious person who enjoys a morning jog. Or a historian who is genuinely intrigued about revealing the mysteries of human history. Or a technology enthusiast who is fascinated about tapping into new capabilities while playing with robotics.

People do respond to incentives. But incentives alone are not enough to change behavior. If it were, any man should be able to walk up to any woman and propose sex for money. But people like to make choices that are within their frame of interest and are in line with their life goals. So, people do not always respond to incentives. And you cannot make a person do what you want so long as an incentive is provided.

People are motivated by money. But you have to provide

more than financial incentives to effectively change behavior. You have to show how making one choice over another is in their best interests before they will voluntarily do it. When workers lose interest in their work, they lose motivation to be productive, even when they are being sufficiently financially compensated. So, if the goal is to improve skills or increase productivity, being a reputable and experienced expert, taking pride in producing high quality work, or producing successful projects, may be more of a motivator and an incentive to work than money itself. With these additional intrinsic motivators in place, people will want to improve their skills or performance because they gain so much more than just a paycheck.

8

Encouragement & Discouragement

Another way to motivate behavior is by encouraging wanted behaviors or discouraging unwanted behaviors. Encouragement instills courage in a person or confidence in a person's abilities. And it can take on many forms, including giving recognition for positive contributions, giving awards, or expressing trust and confidence in a person. Encouragement provides social validation and confirms that those behaviors are wanted and valued. And that encouragement can be emotionally rewarding, and can motivate a person to repeat those behaviors.

Discouragement, on the other hand, expresses disapproval and tends to demotivate behavior. People should be discouraged from activities that could do significant harm or damage. But too much discouragement could have negative effects. For example, if a parent tries to punish a child into submission without ever providing positive feedback, it could cause the child to become discouraged with life in general. Frequently being reminded that you will never amount to anything, could lead to feelings of low self-esteem and low self-confidence, that could have a negative impact on a person's choices later in life.

Encouragement can also be problematic because it depends on how receptive people are to outside influences. Conflict, for example, can prevent a person from being receptive to influence. Teenagers who are trying to establish greater individuality, sometimes conflict with the wishes of their parents. And consequently, they stop being receptive to their parent's advice. So, people need to be trusting and open to influence before they will listen to words of encouragement.

The way people judge us, and our abilities, may be encouraging or discouraging, depending on how receptive we are to that feedback. During the 1960's, Robert Rosenthal, PhD, described an effect, he called the Pygmalion effect, in which expectations about how well a person performs can actually influence that person's performance. If Susan's manager explicitly expresses an expectation that she will perform well because she is a very strong and capable person, then her performance may improve as a result of this added validation and confidence in her abilities.

In 1969, Dr. J. Sterling Livingston further suggested that the effect could be applied to management.[34] For example, when a manager has positive feelings and high expectations of subordinates, they are more likely to have high expectations of themselves. When a manager repeatedly expresses confidence in a worker's abilities, the worker may be encouraged to perform at a higher level. Similarly, how people feel about themselves, and their confidence in their own abilities, can influence their performance.[21]

Role modelling, and learning how to perform a role by observing other people, can also encourage specific behaviors. During the 1960's, Social Learning theorists Albert Bandura, Dorothea Ross, and Sheila Ross, did a series of studies at Stanford University where they collected evidence for how aggressive and non-aggressive role models influence children's behavior. Children assigned the aggressive role models exhibited aggressive behaviors. And children assigned to non-aggressive role models, or no role model at all, exhibited fewer instances of aggressive behaviors.[23] Their research suggested that children who have strong positive role models are more likely to develop positive traits.

Knowing how to encourage children to challenge their abilities, including their intellectual abilities, physical abilities, or social abilities, can further the development of social skills, memory and problem-solving skills, and healthy-life skills. Encouraging a strong desire to take on challenging problems can plant a seed of self-confidence that enables the child to grow into a more confident and resilient adult capable of taking on the challenges of living. In fact, self-confidence, according Psychologist Carol Dweck, may influence personal and financial success far more than intelligence.[15] People who are highly confident in their abilities can have the grit and tenacity to continue trying until the desired result is achieved. And that may translate into better mental resilience during difficult times and improved ability to overcome difficult challenges.

Managers can use encouragement and discouragement as a way to develop human capital within the organization. One dilemma that managers face is that the organization, itself, needs people with specific skills doing specific jobs. If those skills are not present, or are not strong enough to be effective, either performance suffers or management needs to hire outside labor to perform the work. So, one way to take more responsibility for the direction of the organization is by encouraging qualified workers to develop the desired skills. When an organization has the right capabilities and skills, the business not only operates more efficiently, as a result of gains in performance and productivity, it also gets a better return on its labor investment.

9

Commitment

How devoted or dedicated a person is to an activity or an organization, like work, relationships, a career, a hobby, or a cause, could be called one's level of commitment. When people are more committed to the organizations to which they belong, they tend to be more productive, produce higher quality of work, and have a desire to stay with the company longer. In previous sections, we looked at how financial incentives have a limited influence on motivating behavior. But job satisfaction may be even more important in causing an increase or decline in commitment.

Job satisfaction, and the desire to be part of the organization, may be one of the strongest motivators of workplace commitment. Workers who are dissatisfied with their work may be less committed to the organization, less committed to staying productive, less committed to producing high quality work, and more likely to look for work elsewhere. Some of those causes of dissatisfaction may include personal conflicts, a lack of personal acceptance, inadequate training, a lack of clearly defined goals, unfair and harsh treatment, or a lack of appreciation.

So, to eliminate these causes of dissatisfaction, management could provide training programs to advance skills and improve job performance, which reduces mistakes and conflict, and enables workers to take pride in their work. Communicating well-defined goals can help workers to know what they should be striving toward. And policing unethical or harsh behavior can create greater trust of management, and a greater sense of fairness among workers. And showing appreciation for hard work can acknowledge the sacrifices that workers make, to let them know that their work is valued and appreciated.

10
Critical Skills

Project success ultimately depends on effort and productivity. And increasing your productivity can start by improving your cognitive focus and reducing time-wasting distractions that could prevent you from achieving your goal. To do that, try scheduling time to devote exclusively to your project and find ways to eliminate distractions.

Goalsetting provides another way to increase productivity by focusing your thinking and effort on a well-defined course of action. Without clearly defined goals, it becomes difficult to know what you are working toward. Goalsetting further helps you to schedule and manage your time by breaking-down large goals into smaller, more manageable, goals.

Time management has a tremendous influence on productivity. If you try to complete quick and easy tasks first, it will give you more time to focus on more complex tasks, later. You also need to try to create a realistic schedule. To do that, measure the amount of time required to complete a common task. This will create a baseline that you can use to schedule all other tasks. And be patient as you work toward your goals. Sometimes people become impatient and create an unrealistic schedule, which can lead to excessive stress, excessive work demands, mistakes, and failure. Leverage time by breaking down larger, more complex, tasks into smaller more manageable tasks, that you can schedule over a longer period of time. And give yourself extra time for unforeseen events.

If your project requires you to be creative, look at other similar works that have proven to be successful. By drawing ideas from successful projects, rather than simply relying exclusively on your own trial-and-error experimentation, you are more likely to be successful. Model and diagram your ideas on paper. This can help you plan your project, and identify costly mistakes in your project, before you have invested considerable amount of time and energy into building it.

At some point in life, you may find yourself in a role, as a parent, leader, instructor, or coach, where your ability to motivate other people can influence how effective you are. To do that, you not only need to know your target audience and be able to control attention, you need to be able to change expectations. Since choices are heavily influenced by what people expect to gain or lose, changing behavior often requires changing expectations about the available option. And you can do that by explaining why making one choice over another is in their best interests, or enables them to gain more of what they want.

Incentives (e.g., compensating labor or sanctioning prohibited behavior), provides another way to increase productivity, to some extent. People respond to incentives as they strive to make wanted gains or avoid unwanted losses. But incentives, alone, are usually not enough to change behavior, and can sometimes motivate the wrong behaviors. For example, when people begin trying to obtain a reward, or avoid a punishment, at any cost. Some other examples include trying to punish someone into submission, or trying to bribe a person to perform an act. Criminal organizations, like drug cartels, often rely on these types of tactics to influence behavior. People are more likely to cooperate when they believe they are acting in their best interests and are making decisions that are in line with their life goals.

Another way to motivate productivity in organizations is by providing the right types of encouragement and discouragement. Encouragement tells people to increase more of a wanted behavior. And discouragement provides negative feedback that tells a person to decrease an unwanted behavior. But for encouragement or discouragement to be effective, those receiving the advice need to be receptive to feedback. People are often not receptive to feedback for many reasons, often because of a lack of trust or conflict.

Suppose, for example, a manager encourages a worker to develop a skill or take on a difficult challenge. If she succeeds, and she gets credit for her accomplishment, she, along with her coworkers, can see that her effort is wanted, valued, and appreciated by management within the organization. And it creates a goal for other workers to strive toward, knowing that they too will be recognized and rewarded, rather than ignored, for their effort. This can ensure that organizations have the skills necessary to function effectively enough to stay in business.

Within organizations, managers may be able to strengthen the commitment of their workforce by improving job satisfaction. When workers are more satisfied in their jobs, they may be more willing to contribute to making the organization successful. When workers are dissatisfied, they may be more likely to care less about their productivity, or the quality of their work, and more likely to resign. Job satisfaction may be improved with better communication, providing better training in weak areas, establishing clearly defined goals, policing unfair or harsh treatment, and by showing appreciation for hard work and contributions.

This chapter mostly focused on how to motivate yourself and other people to be more productive. But to effectively work with other people, you need to build strong and healthy relationships and motivate people to cooperate toward shared interests. And in the next chapter, we will look at some techniques for doing that.

CHAPTER 9:
MOTIVATING COOPERATION

To be successful at many things in life, you have to cooperate with others in the pursuit of shared or common interests.
The ability to cooperate gives you the power to do much
more than you could ever do alone. Cooperation allows you
to pool resources and effort to accomplish large tasks in a
shorter period of time. And you cannot do many things, like
earn an income, establish a family, or run a business, without the cooperation of those who make it possible. Healthy
relationships not only provide help in times of need, they
provide emotional support, positive experiences, a greater
sense of security, and may give your life greater meaning
and purpose as you are needed by your friends, family, or
coworkers.

This chapter looks at the personal skills and techniques
that strengthen cooperation, like communication skills, conflict resolution skills, the ability to gain trust and confidence. Many of these techniques improve social status, or
what people think about each other, the strength of their relationship, and their willingness to cooperate. Social status
is heavily influenced by the social dynamics of how personal relationships change and evolve overtime as a result
of personal interactions and feelings. Those interactions

change the way people think about each other, their expectations, and how they work together.

1

Healthy Relationships

A *healthy relationship* is one that makes everyone better-off as a result of being in the relationship. You should establish rules for the type of treatment you are willing to accept to protect yourself from harm, or form people who would make you worse off. But at the same time, you need to consider and respect the wants and interests of those in the relationship, even when their interests differ from your own.

Any relationship in which one or more people experience hostility, mistreatment, or unfair losses, is an unhealthy relationship. When conflict continues to escalate, it can create chronic distress that can do increasing mental and physical harm to everyone involved. If that conflict continues to escalate and becomes increasingly hostile with no resolution, it should be ended to protect the safety and welfare of everyone involved.

Ending a relationship, especially one you depend on for your livelihood, can be difficult. Married couples who have children stand to lose a substantial amount of financial support, a standard of living, their child's education, or a retirement. And finding a new partner, whom you can trust and confide in, can be difficult. So, it's important to consider whether its better to try to fix, or end, the relationship.

A possible solution may be to set expectations early, or form an agreement about the conditions upon which the relationship could end. Simply because people have a conflict or disagreement does not necessarily mean it is an unhealthy relationship, or that their differences cannot be reconciled. Sometimes it requires effort on the part of those involved to communicate and confide in each other to work out their differences.

2
Communication Skills

Cooperation and teamwork, requires strong communication skills. And a lack of effective communication skills can cause misunderstandings between people and an inability to cooperate toward shared goals. Non-verbal communication, like your facial expressions, vocal characteristics, posture, and appearance, can create misunderstandings when it does not convey the right mood or intentions. In business, failures in communication can cause organizational dysfunction, business failures, and the inability to identify and resolve problems. Any of these can cause a decline in productivity, a loss of worker satisfaction, client satisfaction, and revenue.

Communication skills are developed just like any other skill, by testing your ability with practice and receiving feedback. Feedback can help you improve communication when it enables you to gain insight into areas where you need improvement that you would, otherwise, overlook. And that feedback can come in the form of body language, emotional and verbal responses, as well as attention and acknowledgment. Listening, itself, is a communication skill that allows people to receive feedback, share ideas, expertise, and to see things from other people's perspective.

How a message is delivered and interpreted can determines how well that message is received. If Sandra disagrees with a new departmental policy and expresses that disagreement by verbally attacking the idea, the audience may take a defensive stance and stop being receptive to the attack. But if she presents the problem as an opportunity for improvement, and shows how everyone benefits from changing the policy, the audience may be more receptive to her different perspective.

3
Emotional Skills

The ability to convey specific emotions, or recognize emotions in others, could be called emotional skills, or emotional intelligence. Liking or disliking something is an emotional reaction of trust or fear, which is part of our intuitive judgment. And that intuitive judgment can change the way people view and interact with each other. The way you make people feel, and the emotions you convey, is a skill that can be developed with practice. And developing those skills requires self-awareness of how you make other people feel and how they interpret your behavior.

People with highly developed emotional skills are able to separate their feelings and perceptions from how they treat other people. If you are upset about a problem, have a low opinion of another person, or are having a rough day, the people you interact with did not do anything to deserve poor treatment because of it. If you allow your feelings and perceptions to influence the way you interact with other people, especially if you are upset about something, your behavior may be interpreted as malicious and threatening and may send the wrong message.

At the same time, it's also important to note that people can experience so much stress that they say things they do not mean. This is more common than people realize. Stress can significantly impair a person's judgment and interfere with decision-making. So, it would be unfair to characterize a person as a one-dimensional character, like some comic-book villain, who has malicious intentions simply because that person is experiencing a great deal of distress. Often when a person is having an emotional experience, that person has underlying problems that you do not see on the surface. Even when an employee is trying to do the right thing for one's employer, if that employee is understaffed and overworked, it can cause distress that changes attitudes and causes them to say, or do, things that are uncharacteristic. If the real source of the problem is being overworked, then putting the blame exclusively on the person experiencing the distress would be an attribution error, and would not resolve the root cause of the problem. But to recognize this problem, you have to separate your own emotional reaction from what you are observing.

Improving cooperation, whether it is with your family or coworkers, also involves learning to reduce words or actions that evoke feelings of conflict, fear, or distress. Anytime problems arise, reassuring people that everything will be fine and then working with them to create a better solution, can be more effective than simply reacting by verbally attacking specific people. Even a glance or a few words can make a person feel threatened, even if that is not the intention. So, to have a strong and healthy relationship, you need to continue building and maintaining that relationship, rather than allowing positive or negative events, or things you like or dislike, to dictate the course of the relationship.

In business, the emotional skills of management can be observed in how managers treat workers, which can influence job satisfaction and productivity. Research has suggested that when workers have low expectations and low confidence in their abilities, those feelings decrease motivation and productivity. Psychologists call this the Galatea effect, or the self-fulfilling prophecy. In other words, when a person has low self-confidence, and a fear of failure, that person is more likely to fail.

Research has also suggested that when management expresses high expectations and high confidence in their worker's abilities, self-confidence and productivity can increase. Psychologists call this the Pygmalion effect, or the power of expectations. When workers are treated like they are capable of succeeding, they are more likely to succeed. When management treats workers like they cannot succeed, that discouragement may prevent them from trying. Or, even worse, when workers are harshly threated, their sense of obligation to the organization may deteriorate, which could negatively influence their attitudes and productivity.

4

Trust

For people to cooperate in a healthy relationship, they have to trust, and believe, that they will act in their interests, rather than acting against their interests. Early in relationships, trust can be lost relatively quickly, and for many different reasons. When a person stops communicating, it can cause cooperation to deteriorate. Or when a person stops taking responsibility for one's decisions and puts blame on others, or does not follow through on promises, can leave problems unresolved or do unintentional harm. And within organizations, workers can begin to lose trust in management for similar reasons, for example, if they fail to police the organization from mistreatment or misuses of power.

In 2012, internet search engine company Google did a

private study they called Project Aristotle, which explored what made the most productive and creative teams. And despite different personality types, what made for the most productive teams were those that created a "safe environment" in which members were allowed to take risks, propose new ideas, and make suggestions in meetings, without being subjected to feelings of negative judgment or harmful criticism.[13]

Teamwork requires trust. People need to be able to depend on their team mates without suspecting that they are working against their interests. When people feel like they, or their ideas, are under constant attack, the instinct is to fight or flee, which can cause cooperation to rapidly deteriorate. So, allowing people to have their own opinions and viewpoints, and acknowledging good ideas, even when they come from people who often do not have the best ideas, can go a long way to build trust.

Another way to build trust is to take your relationships out of a stressful work or home environment, and create opportunities for positive experiences. This allows people relax, drop their defenses, enjoy life, and reveal a different side of themselves. Employers sometimes try to encourage this by having company picnics, or do team building exercises, to encourage more positive experiences, and promote better trust and communication, among workers.

Being friendly and inviting can also improve trust. You do that in your social interactions by having a positive attitude or offering help and assistance. And you can change the environment around you, maybe by including interesting conversational pieces, which can create a friendlier and more inviting atmosphere in which people want to spend time conversing. These techniques many not work for everyone, all the time. But they are more effective than doing nothing at all.

5
Conflict Resolution Skills

Conflict occurs when one or more people take an opposing side in an argument or some disputed topic. Conflict is unavoidable as all people are motivated to protect and defend their interests. And while conflicts can remain friendly and resolvable, they can also escalate into verbal attacks, violence, and destructive behavior. Conflicts may be one of the most destructive forces in cooperative relationships. So ideally, you want to avoid, or mitigate, the damage caused by conflict as much as possible. When people are in a state of conflict, they may not only be motivated to hurt the other person physically, socially, or financially, they can create high levels of chronic distress and tension that causes poor judgment, poor decisions, and unintended consequences.

Ultimately, you are forced to live with the consequences. And winning an argument is not the same as creating the best outcome. So, rather than inflaming tensions, counterattacking, and perpetuating conflict because you are angry at another person, you need to consider whether your actions will actually help you achieve your goal, or will help to improve the outcome you are trying to create.

Many conflicts involve people who have competing interests. And resolving those conflicts may require a compromise. To do that, you need to understand what the other person wants. And a quick, and sometimes counterintuitive, way to evaporate those emotions, is by seeing things from the other person's perspective. People do not listen to their enemies; they listen to their allies. So, you need to get on that person's side to look at things from that person's perspective. You are never going to effectively influence a person by siding against that person. They will always see you as a threat, stand at defense, and be ready to attack.

During my early years working as a customer service representative, this served as a very effective strategy for handling angry customers. Some of my coworkers would argue back-and-forth with customers, telling them "you cannot do that," or "you cannot treat me that way," and sometimes the customer would hang up. My approach was to immediately agree with the customer and attempt to see things from that person's perspective. Rather than caving in and trying to fulfill the customer's every wish, I simply represented the customer as best I could in accordance with company policy. If policy prohibited me from doing something, I explained the reasons. And this approach had a dramatic effect. In a few instances, when a customer would call in angry and screaming, and quickly realized that I was not fighting back on the issue, the person would immediately quite down, apologize, and begin to listen or explain their problem. On several occasions, coworkers verbally accused me of lying and cheating because of my high call-resolution rate.

Conflicts are not always easy to resolve and sometimes may require mediation from a Therapist, Counselor, or a professional who can settle disputes. Sometimes it helps to have someone who is not emotionally involved with the conflict assess everyone's needs and create a compromise that is best for everyone, if that is possible. You also need to be careful in the way you seek mediation. Human Resources people may not help, and may think more in terms of what the company can be sued for if they want to terminate your employment, rather than making an attempt to help you. And in States that have little or no employee protection laws, attorneys may not take your case if they do not think they can win.

6

Critical Skills

To be successful in your life roles, or in striving to achieve your goals, you often need to cooperate and build relationships with those who can help you succeed. To that end, try to build healthy relationships in which everyone is made better-off. Relationships in which you could be harmed, or in which you could harm the other person, would be an example of an unhealthy relationship.

Communication is the means by which relationships form and grow strong. Within organizations, if you do not have strong enough communication, it can cause organizational disfunction, unresolved problems, and failures. So, to keep your relationships strong, you want to make sure that communication is occurring and that any problems are being addressed. This requires strong listening skills, and genuinely trying to understand the other person's perspective. And it requires communicating messages in a way that avoid offending or angering people.

Good communication skills also depend on good emotional skills. Part of having strong emotional skills involves separating your own emotions from the way you treat other people. Strong emotional intelligence also means understanding that when a person is having a negative emotional experience, maybe one is stressed out or is angry, that person may have other underlying problems causing those emotions. And it's important to understand what those problems are before you judge that person.

Trust, and knowing that you can depend on someone to

act in your interests, is a defining part of personal relationships. Part of that trust forms when you allow other people to freely suggest ideas without negative judgment or harmful criticism. People should be allowed to have their own opinions and viewpoints without feeling constantly attacked. And one way to build trust is to create more positive experiences by being friendlier and more inviting, and starting more conversations.

Conflicts can occur in any relationship. Sometimes winning an argument is not the same as creating the best outcome. Ideally, you want to avoid or reduce the amount of damage caused by a conflict. So, rather than stepping up your opposition, it may be more advantageous to see things from the other perspective, so you can work out a compromise.

The next part of this book looks at the effects of stress and adversity on the human condition. Among the many different influences on the human condition, adversity is one of least understood, and most destructive. Not only does adversity create distress that impairs the ability to use good judgment, if severe enough, adversity can even result in certain types of mental disorders.

PART V:
ASSESSING STRESS & ADVERSITY

Human suffering is universal in the human condition as all people experience pain, stress, and adversity. If some theoretical perfect world did exist, it would still have natural disasters, and people would still experience pain, suffering, deprivation, neediness, and want. So, while some forms of suffering may be unavoidable, it may be possible to reduce unnecessary suffering by educating people about different forms of adversity.

Adversity is an antonym for, and the opposite of, support. If we looked at the basic life support systems necessary for survival, it would consist of food, water, and shelter. A lack of any of these would create adversity and distress as you struggle to find the resources necessary for survival. So, adversity, is like a perception that the world is against you, which creates distress. When people experience mild forms of adversity, they often don't feel supported. And that, by itself, can create a significant amount of distress. High levels of distress can influence a person emotionally, in terms of anger or sadness, and can impair judgment in ways that leads to poor life-altering decisions. Some of the more extreme examples would be violent homicidal or suicidal behaviors.

All people experience varying levels of adversity that creates distress in their lives. And in the following chapters, we look at how adversity is one of the most powerful and destructive forces on the human condition and mental health. The following chapters not only explore the negative effects of adversity, or the distress created by that adversity, it offers some approaches to handling distress, in addition to greater insight into how adversity influences the human condition.

In an earlier chapter of this book, we looked at the fact that challenging a person's abilities can make that person stronger or, as the phrase goes: "What does not kill you, makes you stronger." And to some extent, that is true with some forms of adversity. As you confront difficulties in your life, and try to overcome those challenges, your ability to do that can grow stronger. But more severe forms of adversity can also do severe damage that does not always make a person stronger.

Adversity exists on a spectrum, from minor, inconsequential, forms, to severe forms that can drive a person crazy or lead to death. On the low end of adversity spectrum, you have a type of paradise where no adversity exists. On the high end, you have hell-on-earth, which is a very extreme, persistent, and possibly life-threatening. Most people live somewhere in between, some days closer to paradise, and other days closer to hell. And very few people live at the extremes.

Many people in developed economies, like the United States, experience very minor forms of adversity and distress on a daily basis. These are more like minor frustrations and inconveniences, like slow traffic, disagreements over ideas, personal attacks, competitive rivalry, or political disagreements, that may not necessarily damage people's lives.

And then there are more severe forms, like the worker who is treated poorly by his manager, who then goes home and takes his anger and resentment out on his wife and kids. Or people who are discriminated against, based on personal preferences, race, or ethnicity, who may experience unnecessary hostility and unfair losses due to discrimination. And then you have cases concerning basic quality of life issues that cause a decline in a person's condition, like a lack of access to food or clean water.

The longer a person experiences adversity, the greater amount of damage it has the potential to do. In earlier chapters, we looked at how self-confidence can be encouraging and can motivate people to achieve goals. Adversity, by contrast, can be discouraging and can prevent people from taking on challenges or developing in healthy ways. Children who grow up, or live, in environments with frequent instances of adversity, may have developmental deficits, maybe less willing to trust and confide in others, and less able to regulate emotions, all of which put's the child at a significant disadvantage later in life.

The idea that severe forms of adversity can cause mental disorders has a scientific basis. Studies have shown that children who have experienced greater childhood adversity, like child abuse, are known to develop mental disorders as a result of their adverse experiences. People who experience more racial adversity also experience increased instances of mental health problems. And while policy and enforcement can go a long way to reduce forms of adversity in organizations and communities; ultimately, the public needs to be more educated about how adversity negatively impacts people's lives to recognize the problem and change the behavior.

Learning about how adversity affects people mentally, and influences their stress-levels, is critical to human judgment and decision-making. People are often not able to recognize how their own actions unknowingly and unnecessarily create adversity. For example, when people esteem and evaluate other people's qualities based on their own personal values, they may not value those qualities. And that can lead to a low opinion, or negative bias, simply because they are making different life choices. And those positive or negative opinions tend to influence how people are treated and the course of relationships.

In this next chapter, we look at the causes of distress, and some techniques for managing distress. In the final chapter, we look more specifically at the damage caused by severe forms of distress and adversity. It enumerates a few of the common examples of adversity known to negatively impact the human condition, like various types of biases, unemployment, social isolation, or cyber-bullying.

CHAPTER 10:
STRESS MANAGEMENT

As you pursue your life goals, you may find yourself in a constant battle to keep-up with a demanding schedule, constantly responding to the demands of family members, coworkers, or managers. And inevitably, time constraints, personal conflicts and disagreements, and unexpected events, will get in the way and create distress. In this chapter, we look at the negative effects of distress and ways of managing distress so it does not negatively impact your life. And we also look at the influence of judgment on distress, like underestimating the time or skills required, or overestimating the severity of problems.

When people think about stress management, they often think about self-control and emotional attitudes, like how do you handle negativity, difficulties, and frustrations. If people treat you unfairly, or are abusing their privileges, do you respond by flying-off-the-handle in a fit of rage? Do you harbor resentment and spend a lot of time alone, ruminating about those instances in an infinite feedback-loop of escalating anger? Or do you binge drink in the attempt to suppress those feelings? The problem with these behaviors as a way of coping with distress is that they influence your productivity, relationships, and how you perform your roles. So, this chapter looks at some better techniques for handling these problems.

1

Stress Management

Negative forms of stress are not only harmful to a person mental and physical health, it can cause one to make terrible decisions as a result of impaired judgment. So, it's important to have ways to manage that stress, or develop healthy coping skills.

It's not possible to avoid all forms of stress. As you struggle to achieve your life goals, like earning a living, paying bills, or working with different people, you will experience unavoidable distress. And simply walking away from the problems that create distress can do more harm than good. You need a way to increase your mental endurance, which not only includes your ability to handle work, but to endure and be resilient during difficult times. And in later sections, we look at ways to improve your mental toughness and stamina, by changing how you view and handle difficult circumstances.

Not all forms of stress are unhealthy or are harmful. Many healthy stressors tend to improve and reinforce your condition. For example, challenging your abilities and learning a difficult subject are examples of activities that put stress on your mind and body, yet they make positive change by promoting personal growth and development, they strengthen abilities, improve decision-making, and produce wanted outcomes.

Other forms of healthy stress include eustress, which is aroused by stimulating and thrilling activities, like sports or entertainment, and tends to be physically and emotionally beneficial. Some emotional stressors, like anger, can be beneficial when it motivates you to make positive change in your life or a positive difference in the community. Activities that evoke wakefulness, excitement, and exertion are believed to release hormones, like DHEA, which is believed to stimulate brain growth and brain development. These are all beneficial forms of stress that you should seek-out, rather than avoid, if you are striving for personal growth and development.

In managing stress, you not only want to increase positive forms of stress in moderation, you also want to decrease negative, or harmful, forms of stress that can impair judgment and cause poor and impulsive decisions. The American Institute of Stress reported that distress causes crime, violence, unhealthy behaviors, and loneliness, and is responsible for the majority of visits to primary care physicians.[3]

Severe distress impairs judgment, causes emotional instability and impulsive decisions, and generally results in bad, unwanted, behavior. And often, when a person is angry about something that happened to them, for example, if a person were wrongfully accused of something, it can seem to justify that anger and bad behavior. And that justification, especially when one continues repeating the justification, can make the anger and behavior far worse. It's not always easy for people to swallow their pride and their ego and admit that their behavior is the problem, especially when they feel fully justified in their behavior.

Distress does cause a number of behavioral problems, including angry outbursts, unnecessary conflicts, social avoidance, a decline in productivity, reckless driving, and fatal accidents. Distress sometimes causes a sudden end to a long-term relationship, divorces, employee resignations and firings, and in cases, like domestic disputes and retaliation, may require law enforcement intervention. So, the negative effects of distress are very real and impactful and are responsible for many higher-order negative consequences that could be prevented with better stress management.

Problems that create distress can be situational in that they are created by external causes that are beyond your control. Even events that occurred in the past can continue to influence your current situation and create distress. So, one way of reducing that distress is to shift your cognitive focus from your external locus, or things you have no control over, to your internal locus, and things you do have control over. When you begin to experience distress, relax to relieve yourself of tension and emotions that could influence your thinking and cause you to make poor decisions. And then shift your cognitive focus to your own efforts and performance, like staying on task, taking a break, or understanding what you could be doing, or not doing, to create the problems in your life.

2

Fear & Distress

In what is now referred to as the Great Depression, banks were closing and citizens were withdrawing their life savings from their accounts. Knowing that fear only made the situation worse for banks and the entire financial system, the U.S. President Franklin Delano Roosevelt in his 1933 inaugural address, stated "the only thing we have to fear is fear itself."

Fear is one of the most powerful and compelling influences on behavior. Anything that threatens your interests, like a loss of physical safety, a loss of time or money, or missed deadlines, can evoke fear. Even time constraints, and the inability to finish a project on time and within budget, can evoke fear and distress that may compel a person to work faster, or longer hours, to complete the project.

When faced with a threat, you have a few choices: You could combat the threat, escape the threat, or play dead. This lower instinctual response, sometimes called the fight-or-flight response, influences how you engage or avoid the challenges presented by circumstances. These responses can be minor, like avoiding, or conflicting with, certain people or situations. And they can be extreme, like acts of homicide to annihilate a threat, or suicide in flight from the terrors and hardships of living.

Fear is also a paradoxical emotion in that it can work for you, or work against you, depending on how you respond. Fear works for you when it keeps you safe, helps you assess when situations are too risky, and compels you to behave responsibly. Fear about potential future outcomes (i.e., destitution, poverty, or loneliness), compels people to be productive, develop skills, seek employment, and develop beneficial relationships. So, in many ways, fear about future outcomes can motivate you to be more responsible and dependable, and can enable you to make decisions that prevent loss and hardship.

But fear can also work against you, especially if you overestimate the severity of your circumstances, which some people call: "Making a mountain out of a molehill." People can live in terrible situations. But how they learn to handle those situations is part of what influences the consequences they live with. Does one become flighty or combative, which tends to impair thinking, judgment, and rational decision-making? Does one retreat from the problems of living, or respond with extreme aggression to everyday circumstances? These reactions can cause a lot of damage.

The problem with fear is that when you increase fear, you also increase distress, which is known to impair judgment and decision-making. If you can decrease fear, you can also decrease distress, so that you can think more clearly as you work toward solving the problem you face. Some of this involves learning how to relax, reduce fear and anxiety, and focus on your performance. Some people call this ability "performing under pressure," in which you are put into an uncomfortable and distressing situation, but exercise enough self-control to perform at a high level.

3

Stressors

Every day, you are surrounded by stressors that include experiences, events, or memories that can put stress on you mentally and physically, which could include long lines at a store, traffic congestion, or workplace demands. Physical stressors often create muscle tension and injuries, and mental stressors can result in emotional disturbances.

Human judgment, and how people perceive and estimate the severity of their circumstances, has a tremendous effect on their stress levels. In the previous section, we looked at how people sometimes overestimate the severity of their circumstances. For example, when you look at a problem, or obstacle that stands in the way of achieving a goal, do you perceive it as impossible and insurmountable, or is it relatively doable with effort and perseverance? In the first case, when you see your circumstances as impossible, it can cause your stress level to escalate. Viewing the same problem as doable can help you stay calm, collected, and deescalate your stress levels, so that you can think clearly enough to consider your options and solve problems. The ability to avoid panic, and overexaggerating the severity of a problem, is a coping skill can prevent unnecessary conflict and tension.

This can become more difficult as the adversity you experience increases. More severe stressors are created by experiences that significantly threaten you, or are hurtful or damaging to things you care about, and want to protect and defend. Some people call these character defining moments because they are the circumstances in which people demonstrate whether they can handle the pressure. In these circumstances, people sometimes draw on their concept of a strong character, if they have one. For instance, do they put on a strong exterior, and not let petty disputes or minor aggravations get the best of them? This example of a strong character can be instrumental in enabling you to handle life problems. But it can also have limitations in that you need to be realistic about the amount of distress and adversity a person is capable of handling.

4

Chronic Stress

Many career-minded people experience elevated levels of stress on a daily basis. You may be constantly responding to work-related demands, working excessive hours, or are responding to threats to your employment or physical safety. These heightened levels of distress that occur on a daily basis cause chronic stress, which is known to have a detrimental impact on your health. Chronis stress increases your heart rate and releases stress hormones, which can result in harmful wear and tear on the mind and body that has been called allostatic load.[40]

A common example of chronic stress is when a worker is trying to handle the workload of several people. Employers sometimes underestimate the amount of labor or skill required to perform a job. And when a person is overworked as a result of being short staffed, it can create unrealistic demands on that person. And that can increase stress levels and the potential for conflict, which can cause people to make impulsive, terrible, and career ending decisions. This is one of the reasons employers, and human resources people, need to look into reports, rather than simply firing someone, because that report may actually point to an underlying problem with staffing that management is unaware of.

Chronic stress, according to studies, has a variety of symptoms including emotional and behavioral problems, finger biting, emotional instability, altered eating and sleeping patterns, the use of alcohol or other drugs, and in some instances law enforcement intervention.[9] So, being able to recognize chronic stress in your life, and figuring out ways to mitigate that stress, can help you avoid a decline in your mental and physical health.

When negative forms of distress are experienced frequently enough, they can do damage to the brain and body. Fears and worries, for example, tend increase heart rate and breathing, and mobilize the body for action, all of which places greater demand on the body's internal systems to work harder and move faster. During a stressful event, the nervous system discharges hormones from the endocrine glands, including the hypothalamus, adrenal, and pituitary glands, which are responsible for survival instincts, like emotions, alertness, excitement, aggression, and metabolism. After a distressing episode, the body activates the parasympathetic nervous system to restore homeostasis and stabilize bodily functions and return the body back to its normal stress levels.

When these stress reactions are repeated frequently enough to be considered chronic, they can be linked to psychosomatic disorders, which are physical illnesses caused by alterations in biological function, body chemistry, immune suppression disease, and other diseases. Stress causes muscle tension, increases heart rate and blood pressure, blood sugar rises, blood is directed away from the gut where it is normally needed for digestion, and clots more easily. The American Institute of Stress has said that chronic stress may lead to hypertension, heart attacks, strokes, diabetes, and other problems.[4]

Chronic stressors can originate as persistent threats that create adversity on a regular, maybe daily, basis, like school bullies or abusive managers. Social biases can create persistent threats, if you constantly feel discriminated against, or have some negative bias against you. These persistent threats can change thinking and behavior, and the way people approach circumstances, as they worry about threats, try to avoid or defend themselves from threats, or prepare themselves for future threats. And these mental adjustments created by persistent attacks, like a hostile work environment or abusive behavior, can lead to a decline in mental health. So, recognizing behaviors or circumstances that create chronic distress can improve the mental health of the workforce.

5

Stress Management Techniques

You can use a variety of stress management techniques for

managing and reducing stress. According to stress management experts, you may be able to proactively manage stress by managing your time more effectively. For example, plan things out in advance to prevent unnecessary distress caused by being late for deadlines or missed appointments. Experts also recommend creating realistic expectations, getting enough sleep, developing satisfying relationships, and avoiding too much confrontation and argument.[39]

Your cognitive focus, and what you are currently thinking about, and attending to in the moment, can have a tremendous influence on your stress levels. Suppose you are home alone and find yourself thinking about people or events that make you angry. If you continue dwelling on those things, you may either find yourself ruminating in a toxic pool of escalating anger, or you may take lots of vacations or binge-watch television to escape the stress, neither of which really helps your situation.

One stress management technique for controlling stress, mentioned earlier, involves relaxing and staying on task, or relaxing and taking a break. Reducing distress not only requires you to relax, you have to change your focus to a different activity, like talking to people, reading a book, or doing a chore. Some people say that these activities are therapeutic because they keep your mind from wandering into negative thoughts.

Different activities elicit different thoughts and emotions. So, avoid thoughts that elicit distressing emotions by scheduling your day with activities that improve your condition, in some way, like pursuing life goals. Making positive changes in your life can be rewarding and can improve your overall life satisfaction.

6
Accepting Loss

In earlier chapters, we looked at how people are motivated to pursue their private interests to gain more of what they want. In many instances, doing that can be very stressful because it is like fighting many small battles. If you want a beautiful garden, you need to attack the weeds, the overgrown bushes, and plant more flowers. And sometimes when you push a little harder, you can get exactly what you want. But other times, you have to cut your losses and move on.

People sometimes use different types of character defenses to avoid accepting losses. For example, they may resort to lying or cheating to avoid negative consequences. And when a person is dishonest as a way to make gains, or avoid losses, it can hurt the person credibility, and one's ability to be trusted and believed.

People also tend to become frustrated and angry when they do not get what they want, and attack the obstruction. Not all battles are worth fighting. And fighting a losing battle may not be in your best interest if doing so puts you in a worse situation, or causes other people harm. Fighting a losing battle can cause emotions to escalate, which can impair your judgment and cause you to make terrible decisions that leave you worse-off.

You cannot avoid taking risks. As you strive to make gains, you will experience losses. And while you should try to mitigate losses, you should not necessarily regret or become angry about those losses. Not even the most powerful person on Earth can have everything. At some point, you have to cut your losses and move on to something more productive.

7
Positive Thinking

A positive and optimistic view on life can help reduce distress and improve your overall health and wellbeing. A negative or pessimistic view can create negative emotions and self-doubt that can diminish your self-confidence and cause you to doubt your abilities, give-up on important life goals, or avoid beneficial interactions.

Positive thinking is not the same as avoiding negative issues. People sometimes want to stay positive by ignoring problems hoping they go away or pretend they do not exist. Or, as some people say, they "paint their ship gold." But pretending that problems do not exist does not make them go away. Instead, it allows them to fester and grow worse overtime. That's why, instead of ignoring problems and hoping they go away, people should recognize and take responsibility for resolving problems.

All people have negative experiences. You may be criticized or have harsh comments made about your decisions. You may experience a significant loss, like the loss of a loved one. You may be the victim of another person's irresponsible actions, which can leave you dwelling on those negative experiences. And that negative energy puts a person in a negative state of mind that perpetuates more negative and pessimistic thoughts that can create distress, anger, social avoidance, and despair. This state of mind can reduce your productivity and harm your personal relationships.

Positive thinking plays a role in resilience, and your ability to recover from a negative state of mind, not only by thinking optimistically about the future, but by being able to forgive and see beyond the losses you are not able to get back. Those losses are "water under the bridge" as some people say and dwelling on those losses does not help. If you continue to dwell on negative thoughts, it can prevent you from making wanted gains, in terms of healthy and productive personal relationships. Even in the toughest situations, positive thinking can enable you to see opportunities that lead to positive life experiences and relationships.

8

Attitude

Positive thinking can also reinforce positive attitudes, which can reduce the stress levels in the people around you. Daily life problems and negative experiences can create distress, anger, frustration, and other negative emotional states that can influence your attitude. You may be under a great deal of pressure at work, or had a negative experience with someone close in your life. And those negative experiences can put you in a negative state of mind, which can influence how you interact with people. Allowing your distress to influence your attitude towards people, can create distress in their lives and negatively influence their willingness to help and cooperate with you.

In business, the way managers and coworkers communicate with each other can influence their attitudes. For example, when a problem arises, a manager may put blame on subordinates, or criticize subordinates for mistakes or failures. Sometimes when workers make mistakes or fail, it's because they do not know management expectations. In those circumstances, clearly communicating expectations and providing remedial training can help. When managers create solutions that are better for everyone, especially the workers they depend on, it reduces distress and conflict, and can improve attitudes collectively.

Suppose Tim runs a software development business and one of his clients wants a refund because his employees did not deliver the product in the agreed amount of time. Tim is angry and sends out an email to his development team asking why he's paying them to lose clients and threatening to fire people. Tim's email did not help the situation. Rather than motivating the team to find a solution, his blame pitted team members against each other and made them fearful of losing their jobs. Later, Tim realized his mistake and got with his development team to figure out what went wrong, so they could learn from their mistakes and prevent them from occurring in the future.

9

Recreation

To create a positive state-of-mind, it helps to have positive experiences and positive relationships to reinforce those positive feelings. These activities may consist of relaxation, entertainment, reading a book, or physical activities. Since, you cannot avoid all of life's problems that create distress, recreational activities help to temporarily escape from stressful experiences to create a positive state of mind.

Recreational activities can also have other benefits. They help you reenergize, reduce fatigue, think more clearly, and make better decisions. Leisure and physical activities, like exercise or games, can prevent, and help you recover from, stress related injuries. Spending time with other people can alleviate distress and provide emotional and social reinforcement, which can improve your communication skills and emotional attitudes.

Temporary breaks during the day can be recreational.

That is especially true when work related stress has you considering whether to quit your job. Consider a colleague of mine, Jerry, a software engineer who spends much of his day writing and debugging code. One day, he pounded on his desk and exclaimed: "What is wrong with this stupid thing!" He pounded keys on his keyboard, made frustrated grunts, and uttered annoyed remarks. He was trying to fix a bug in a program but did not know what was causing it. He thought the program should work, but for some un-known reason it did not. Jerry's stress and frustration only slowed his progress as he became angrier. He called it a piece of crap and attacked the problem in the wrong ways, which did not help him solve the problem any quicker. When noticing Jerry's frustration, I asked him to join me for a game of Table Tennis in the recreation room. After a few sets, we were both happier and Jerry was smiling. And within a couple of minutes, Jerry exclaimed he figured out the problem that stumped him.

Research has shown that people who spend extended periods of time trying to solve complex problems can expe-rience a type of cognitive fatigue where parts of the brain responsible for problem solving actually grow tired. Your brain and body both need rest to recuperate energy during extended periods of activity. And taking a break every once-in-a-while allows the brain and body to recover from stress that can cause fatigue and impaired thinking, so you can be productive and effectively tackle the challenges you face.

Meditation can also help people who are highly produc-tive and experience high levels of distress, or when lots of people demand your attention and you need to get away and relax. Not being able to relax can make it difficult to think clearly, make good decisions, and sleep. So, the prac-tice of Meditation, in a way, trains the brain to shut down, on-demand, and relax. Meditation usually involves clearing the mind of residual thoughts and emotions by redirecting your cognitive focus to an activity, like breathing.

10
Critical Skills

Heightened levels of distress can impair judgment, as a result of fear and emotions, and can cause a person to make poor decisions that have negative consequences. For example, when fear causes a person to overestimate the severity of a problem, that person may take drastic actions, which makes the situation worse. So, you should actively try to manage and reduce stress, especially chronic distress that occurs on a regular basis, to reduce the possibility of long-term severe damage to your mind, body, and social life.

One stress management technique for managing and reducing distress involves managing your time more effectively, and planning things in advance, which can prevent you from worrying about, or becoming frustrated by, time deficits and deadlines. You also want to keep a check on your fears. Fear and distress tend to be tightly coupled in that the greater fear you have, the more likely you are to experience distress that could impair your judgment and cause you to make poor decisions. So, trying relax and focus your attention on activities that are productive or recreational can be therapeutic and can help you regain a positive mental state. As you strive to obtain the things you want in life, you will also experience losses along the way. And you need to be willing to accept losses and move on to more productive and fruitful endeavors, rather than responding with all-out-war to every obstruction.

Thinking positively, and having a positive and optimistic view on life, can reduce distress and improve your overall mental health. This does not mean that you simply ignore problems and pretend they do not exist. But it does mean that you do not dwell on, or become discouraged by, negative experiences. Even when you are experiencing adverse events, try to have a positive attitude toward others so you can maintain positive interactions, healthy relationships, and mutual cooperation. Recreation, and spending time away from stressful activities, can also help reduce stressful thoughts that can compound your stress throughout the day. Enjoyable activities, like relaxation, entertainment, or physical exercise, can help you regain a positive state of mind that can improve your experience, ability to endure stress, and strengthen relationships.

Therapy can be beneficial if you are experiencing chronic distress, especially if you are experiencing a decline in your mental or physical health, or are having problems with emotional instability, declining productivity, strained relationships, sleep deprivation, trauma, and addictions.

As you pursue your life goals, you will experience, at least, minor forms of adversity that can create distress. Severe forms of adversity can create distress that has longer-term, more severe, residual lingering effects that can harm your mind and body, and cause a variety of disorders. And in the next chapter, we look at some of these more severe forms of adversity that can be harmful to your mental health.

CHAPTER 11:
MENTAL HEALTH

All people experience various forms of adversity, in different amounts, during their lives. So, it's not surprising to see that many world religions, like Buddhism, make human suffering, and it's causes, an important focal point. Or why Monotheistic religions have a concept of evil, which is often attributed to extremely malicious or hostile actions taken against people. Both human suffering and acts of evil are forms of adversity that create distress and have a very negative impact on people's lives. And in their more extreme or prolonged forms, it can cause a person's mental health and overall condition to decline.

People are, no doubt, far better-off when they are able to be resilient in overcoming adversity. Some minor forms of adversity, like being told you are not a great performer, may even challenge and strengthen your abilities, or inform your judgment onto a better career path. Adversity can positively influence development when it challenges a person's abilities, pushes one to try harder to overcome an obstacle, and causes one to grow stronger as a result. Many life lessons can be learned from negative experiences that force you to reach deep within yourself and try harder to do things you normally would not.

But adversity can also be one of the most destructive forces on a person's mental health. And in this chapter, we look at the reasons why. We look at the mental effects of adversity, why it creates distress, how it discourages development, and why it leads to poor decisions. This chapter also looks at some different forms of adversity that people should be able to recognize, including harmful biases, mistreatment and abuse, loneliness, unemployment, significant social and economic losses, and conflicts, to name a few.

Part of the problem we face is that people often do not understand the adversity they create in other people's lives. Sometimes people are treated poorly because they are different, have different values, different problems that are difficult to understand, or a different way of life. In fact, people often try to leverage political systems against people who they see as a threat to their way of life. People, at one time, created laws enforcing the segregation of people of different races, or banning gay marriage. But simply because a person has a different way of life does not mean it poses a threat. Promoting *egalitarian values*, where people of different ways of life and different values, can be accepted, may reduce those forms of adversity.

1

Mental Effects of Adversity

Adversity effects people in different ways. And how much adversity effects a person mentally, partly depends on how severe the adversity is. On the low end of the adversity spectrum, you have harmless forms of adversity, like a single verbal attack or daily events that cause minor stressors and frustrations. Recovering from these events may only take minutes and may be forgotten about the next day.

On the high end of the adversity spectrum, you have actions that cause serious harm or, if experienced over a prolonged period of time, could have serious long-term effects. Severe forms of adversity can create heightened levels of distress that can be toxic to a person's mental health. A person who was horribly victimized regularly, for example, may experience emotional disturbances, like anger, distrust, or inconsolable sadness, which can impair a person's judgment and cause the person to make poor and impulsive decisions. Repeated exposure to negative experiences can create negative memories and residual emotions that accumulate over a period of time, which may influence trust in personal relationships, or emotional stability if those memories continue to affect a person mentally.

Adversity tends to also negatively influence personal development and productivity. When a person is constantly coping with, or handling, severe forms of adversity, it prevents that person from developing in other, more beneficial, ways. Children who have experienced significant adversity and discouragement from adults or peers may become discouraged to the point of being unproductive and giving up. Examples include a parent telling a child that he is worthless and will never amount to anything on a regular, daily, basis. The child, not knowing what to believe, may believe it and fail to develop healthy life skills for becoming a functioning and independent adult. Not only can a person become completely discouraged about one's own abilities, that person may lose trust in other people, which may diminish a person's social and financial outlook and lead to a state of despair.

2

Childhood Adversity

As a child's brain develops, whether that child is developing in normal and healthy ways can have a tremendous impact on that child's future. Young children are least capable of taking responsibility for the course of their lives for a number of reasons. They do not possess the knowledgebase of life experience required to understand the consequences of their decisions. And they do not possess the skills and resources required to independently financially support themselves. Much of their lives are at the mercy of caregivers and adults who look after their safety, development, and wellbeing. So, anytime a child experiences maltreatment or neglect, it can be harmful to that child's development in ways the child is helpless to do anything about.

Adversity, and severe forms of child maltreatment from parents or peers, effects people from every economic background. And studies going back to before 1998 have shown how a greater number of *Adverse Childhood Experiences* (ACEs) increased the number of risk factors for the leading causes of adult deaths. ACEs include physical abuse, emotional abuse, sexual abuse, or neglect, in addition to various forms of household dysfunction, like mental illness, parental incarceration, substance abuse, and divorce. Participants interviewed in the studies, with greater than four ACEs, were at greater risk of alcoholism, drug abuse, depression, suicide, and other unhealthy conditions.[57]

In 2015, JAMA Pediatrics did a study on Behavioral Risk Factors in the State of Wisconsin that compared the lifelong health outcomes of people who reported more Adverse Childhood Experiences with people who reported more

Positive Childhood Experiences (PCEs). PCEs consist of experiences, like talking to family about difficult topics, feeling supported by friends and family, enjoying community activities, feeling a sense of belonging in school, and feeling safe in their home. In their study, participants who recalled a greater number of ACEs had "changes in brain anatomy, gene expression, and delays in social, emotional, physical, and cognitive development lasting into adulthood." People who reported experiencing more ACEs had an increased risk of adult depression and a lack of social and emotional support that contributed to poorer physical and mental health in adulthood. In contrast, adults who recalled more instances of PCEs before the age of 18, had fewer instances of mental and physical health problems in adulthood. Since PCEs have positive lifelong consequences for mental and physical development in children and adults, researchers argue that greater attention needs to be given to creating more positive experiences for children in the community that can foster better resilience and healthy life outcomes.[8] These studies suggest that reducing Adverse Childhood Experiences and creating more Positive Childhood Experiences may not only reduce risk factors associated with mental decline and physical illness in adulthood, it could reduce the unnecessary costs that burden communities associated with mental health care, incarceration, accidents, and other mental-health-related social problems.

Child maltreatment exists in many forms, including physical abuse, sexual abuse, child exploitation and corruption, emotional abuse, and neglect, all of which are known to cause developmental problems. Emotional abuse, according to American Humane, is known to cause problems with a child's conduct, as well as cognitive disorders, affective disorders, and other mental disorders.[2] Forms of emotional abuse may consist of calling the child something other than his or her name. The caregiver may verbally assault the child by ridiculing, verbally threatening, belittling, or bullying the child. The caregiver may terrorize the child by creating unrealistic expectations and threatening physical harm if the child doesn't live up to those expectations. And the caregiver may isolate the child, to prevent the child from interacting with people, which could reveal the abuse.

Children who were emotionally abused, characteristically, have persistent feelings of insecurity, problems forming relationships, a low self-worth, and self-destructive behaviors. The unstable environment created by an abusive caregiver can disrupt learning and cause emotional disorders that prevent the development of normal cognitive abilities, and can prevent the child from pursuing normal life goals. Older children with more severe emotional disorders may use substances to self-medicate those disorders, or may avoid people in general, including activities that promote healthy growth and development. These effects profoundly influence a person's life choices, like social activity, drug use, and educational attainment.

Abuse can occur for any number of reasons. A parent may become frustrated with a child's behavior and may increase punishment if the child does not respond according. This also happens when caregivers have emotional, anger-related, disorders and inflict uncontrollable violence. When those acts are repeated, unapologetically, it creates a mutually hostile relationship between the caregiver and child, where the child is constantly predicting, preparing for, and reacting to the parent's hostile behavior. These conflicts may be difficult, if not impossible to observe, if the parents are striving for social approval and behave differently around different people. The child may even hide the abuse to avoid losing the caregiver's support, and to avoid violent threats made by the parent if the behavior is revealed.

A caregiver's behavior has an influence on the child's development in other ways. When a parent only punishes or disapproves of the child, that child never learns better ways to handle problems or more constructive social skills. When a child is constantly responding to threats, is kept in a constant state of fear, sadness, or anger, it does not allow for the development of healthy personal skills. Instead of being cooperative, the child learns to be suspicious, defensive, and protective. And that lack of constructive social skills can interfere with future relationships with peers, instructors, and other adults.

During childhood, severe adversity from a parent or peer who continues to create a hostile environment on a regular or daily basis can cause developmental problems. Just as an ability can be further developed, it can also be prevented from developing by isolating a person, preventing a person from interacting with people, keeping a person in conflict, or imposing control over the person's behavior and life choices. Rather than developing normal, healthy, mental and social abilities, the victim may develop social avoidance, skills deficits, and other behavioral problems. Feelings of discouragement as a result of harsh treatment can cause persistent thoughts of giving-up and suicide, or believing that one is never good enough. Children with emotional disorders may struggle more academically, especially if the child has serious depression, or suicidal thoughts, which influence motivation and educational attainment. Consequently, the child may develop strong feelings of anger or depression that distorts perceptions and leads to self-destructive or hostile behavior in place of, otherwise, healthy life skills. All of these influence that child's long-term life decisions.

Contrary to the popular idea of the maternal instinct, and the idea that mothers always protect their young and would never harm them, abusers may be more incentivized to be dishonest and deny abuse, to avoid condemning accusations. In fact, an abuser may create the appearance of having a maternal instinct, or may create an appearance of unconditionally supporting the child. But instead of taking responsibility for the abusive behavior, the caregivers put the blame on the child to show how the child is always at fault. And that may not be difficult since the child may have mental disorders, behavioral problems, poor academic performance, or substance abuse, as a result of living in the abusive environment.

Abused children who have emotional disorders also tend to be confused with spoiled children. People may attribute the child's crying to an unfulfilled demand when, in fact, it is an emotional disorder cause by maltreatment. Sadly, that assumption leads to more mistreatment by adults or peers who bully the child. People who have emotional disorders, by the definition of the disorder, cannot control their emotions and, in some cases, seek substances to sedate those emotions. And self-medication with illegal drugs can lead to criminal behaviors that can result in law enforcement intervention.

Interventions do help and save lives, but mostly in cases where parents are committing other crimes, or the child has physical injuries from the abuse. That is not always the case when an abuser is not guilty of other crimes, keeps a clean home, or is striving for social approval. And that creates an impossible situation for the child who is not mentally, emotionally, or socially prepared for challenges they face, and are unable to make sense out of what is happening. The child's prefrontal cortex is not fully developed. So, the natural response is to fight-or-flee, to avoid the attack or counter-attack. These fight-or-flight responses to short-term conflicts can cause the child to make poor decisions that do not consider the long-term consequences. If the child is under constant verbal attacks from adults or peers, and tries to fight-back, that rebellion may become so exaggerated that it develops into criminal behaviors.

Once a child grows into adulthood, that person is legally responsible for one's behavior, even if that person is not responsible for creating the emotional problems, developmental deficits, and abnormal mental conditions that resulted from the child abuse. This troubled past can haunt a child into adulthood. People often judge others based on their personal history when making decisions about friends, dating, and hiring. People who appear to have a troubled past, like poor academic performance in grade school, may be at a disadvantage in comparison to those who do not. Hiring managers, may make a judgment about a job candidate's natural aptitude, and ability to perform the work, based on previous academic performance.

Societies that do not understand developmental problems often tend to seek quick and easy solutions, like punishment for behavioral problems or medication for mental disorders. And those techniques can be effective, depending on how they are administered and in what circumstances. But a more effective, long-term, solution for those problems involves developing life skills that enable people to be more effective in their life roles. That can provide people who lacked positive role models, or had mental disorders from abuse or neglect, or developmental deficits as a result of "slipping through the cracks," a better, and fairer, chance at a future. Without some guidance in this area, many of those people are at greater risk of being unemployed, incarcerated, or dead at a young age.

3

Harmful Biases

A *bias* is an inclination to favor one thing over another, which influences preferences, likes, interests, wants, and values. People like to use their intuition to form quick judgments based on a small amount of information, like a superficial detail, a positive or negative comment, skin color, or employment status. This leads to forming judgments and making decisions, without considering other underlying facts, which can lead to errors and mistakes in decision-making. And those mistakes can not only be factually wrong, they can be morally and ethically wrong if they cause adversity or harsh treatment.

In earlier chapters, we look at how biases develop as people discover their own preferences, and are influenced by family, friends, and life experiences. This leads people to develop their own view of the world and how it works. Seeing is believing when it comes to beliefs about what is true or not. And when a person has a negative experience, it can be difficult for some to believe that experience even happened. And that can cause adverse treatment as a result of not being believed, or being considered crazy, hallucinating, overexaggerating, or catastrophizing events.

People, as they pursue their private interests, tend to evaluate others, or their decisions, based on their own experiences and personal values. But when others do not represent their values, it can lead to a low opinion, or negative judgment, of those people, which can influence how they are treated. In fact, people sometimes weaponize negative biases against other people for their own selfish purposes. An example of this is in political elections where candidates frequently try to create a negative bias against their political opponents. One candidate may call a political opponent names, try to ruin the person's credibility, or make outrageous accusations to pit the public against the person. And since the public is forced to make decisions based on a very small amount of information, that weakness in judgment can be easily exploited to their advantage.

Even superficial characteristics can bias a candidate's chances in an election. To study this, Psychologist Alexander Todorov did a study where he asked participants to compare portraits of different candidates seeking election in the House or Senate, and to judge the competency of those candidates. The participants predicted the election's outcome more than 70% of the time, suggesting that facial features, rather than qualifications or expertise, may bias voter's judgment of candidates. These types of biases, he suggested, may also influence hiring or promotion decisions.[29]

Ingroup biases, and group affiliation, can have a powerful influence as people strive for social acceptance. Within social groups, insiders can develop ingroup biases where they engage in cronyism, nepotism, and groupthink. And they tend to discriminate, marginalize, and scapegoat outsiders. Anytime a person's way of life is different, or consists of different preferences, wants, and values, people can feel threatened by that different way of life. And when people feel threated, they have the urge to exclude or punish those people, or create laws banning their activities.

Hate brings out of worst of people. It leads to violence, murders, and shootings. And sometimes, negative biases against certain people, or groups of people, can escalate into hate. Historically, negative biases were used to marginalize groups of people, like racial and ethnic minorities. For example, Adolf Hitler, who came to power in Germany after 1933, created a "Reich Ministry of Public Enlightenment and Propaganda," which attempted to use the arts, film, radio, education, and the press to disseminate false information about, and justify hostile actions against, Jewish people. Films, like the Eternal Jew, depicted Jewish people as "subhuman" and parasites that were creating disorder. Newspapers printed antisemitic cartoons. And innocent Jewish people, who were later killed in Nazi gas chambers, were forced to write postcards to send home showing how well they were begin treated.[56]

In the United States during the 1800s, many Caucasian people believed that Africans were primitive humans who were less evolved and were, often, viewed as savages. From the 1920s to the 1950s, African Americans were often caricatured in cartoons and played the role of servants in movies and on television. Productions created for white audiences would use African Americans as comic relief by portraying them in ridiculous stereotypical ways. Much of this propaganda can still be found at the Jim Crow Museum of Racist Memorabilia.[17]

In recent decades, a large number of studies of African Americans, Asian Americans, and Latin Americans, have found that racial adversity, and racism, has a negative effect on people's mental and physical health. According to their studies, the stress created by racial adversity during a prolonged period of time, can elevate blood pressure, weaken the immune system, which puts a person at greater risk for long-term mental and physical health conditions. People who experience racism report more instances of stress, depression, anxiety, and suicidal thoughts. People who experience racism had greater risk of hypertension, unhealthy habits, like smoking or substance use, and chronic conditions, like heart disease and kidney disease.[32]

What makes this problem much worse is that different people, who have different perspectives on the world, have different beliefs about how widespread these problems are. In a study from the Society for Human Resource management, 49% of black HR professionals believed that racial or ethnic discrimination existed in their workplace, whereas, only 13% of their white coworkers agreed. 35% of black workers said that racial inequality exists in their workplace, and only 7% of their white coworkers agreed.[28]

We could certainly speculate why these differences exist, starting with the fact that white participants are not as likely to observe racial discrimination. In fact, this is true for any social problem. If you do not experience the problem first hand from your perspective, you may be less inclined to believe it occurs at all, and more likely to down-play its significance. In many cases, you have to see it to believe it. In other words, the popular phrase holds true that "you can't understand someone until you've walked a mile in their shoes." And if you never see racial bias because you are white, the existence of that bias may not conform to your beliefs about its existence.

Sadly, these different perspectives lead to false beliefs that the world is fundamentally just and that people get what they deserve. If a person did nothing wrong, but is treated very differently, people tend to automatically believe that person must have done something terrible to deserve it. And that biased belief only perpetuates more hardship, fewer opportunities, and unfair discrimination. A common example of this is homelessness. Many people explicitly believe that homeless people are in their terrible situation because they do not want to work, which only perpetuates more homelessness.

Harmful biases are not limited to race or ethnicity. People also create biases that involve weight, physical appearance, unemployment, and financial status, which also causes people to be treated differently, or discriminated against. And it's possible that people who are discriminated against for these reasons may experience some of the same mental and physical health related problems as those who experience racism.

These types of harmful biases can also occur in professions where the professionals have a significant impact on other people's lives. An example of this is when a police investigation results in convicting the wrong person. Logically, suspects that are easier to build a case against are more likely to have committed the crime. But detectives can go too far when they continue building a case against the wrong person, usually because the detective is convinced that the suspect is guilty and focuses on finding more evidence to secure a conviction. Suspects who are not fully mature adults, or people who have learning disabilities, or people who are impaired by drugs or alcohol, may even confess to the crime after being subjected to an exhausting interrogation and promised a reduced sentence, or the ability to prove one's innocence later.[26]

4

Employment Adversity

People can also experience adversity in the workplace for a number of reasons. Even competitive rivalry, itself, can be a form of adversity where people are trying to edge out the competition in vying for the same employment or promotional opportunities. Consequently, a person may behave dishonestly and lie about one's accomplishments or coworkers to get ahead. Or a manager may avoid hiring someone who is more skilled and qualified, who could be a better replacement.

Stress in the workplace not only negatively impacts the health and productivity of workers, it negatively impacts the organization itself. In a telephone pole by Harris Interactive, 35 percent of participants said that their jobs were harming their physical or emotional health. About 42 percent said that their job pressures were interfering with their personal relationships. Nearly a fifth of workers, said that they were aware of physical or verbal bullying in the workplace in the previous year, which created higher stress levels, lower satisfaction, and negative views of the workplace. And about 48 percent said that they had excessive work demands or unreasonable deadlines.[20]

According to the National Institute for Occupational Safety and Health, some of the conditions that potentially create distress included having a heavy workload, working long hours, uncertain job expectations, too much responsibility, and infrequent breaks. Sometimes employers underestimate the skill or labor required to perform a role, which can cause one or more workers to be overworked, or have excessive work demands that would normally be handled by more people. Increased stress was also associated with management style, poor communication, and a lack of help or support from coworkers or managers. Perceiving job insecurity, or lacking opportunity for growth, advancement, or promotion, was also associated with job-related stress.[42]

Managers are humans like all other people. They make

mistakes, have shortcomings, experience problems handling stress, lie to avoid negative consequences, and do not always behave responsibly. The question is, what does management do to respond to these instances. Do they have special protections that exempt them from the consequences of their own behavior, especially if they were hired or promoted for reasons other than skills or credentials, like family or friendship relationship, race, age, or marital status? In "At-Will" employment states, employees are often required to sign a contract stating that their employment can be terminated for any reason. So, management may simply terminate the person's employment for filing a report about coworkers or management. In many states, even when the person was fired for filing a complaint, that person may have no legal recourse to do anything about it.

Studies have shown that employment stress can also be harmful to a person physically and emotionally, as workers who report high stress levels have greater health care expenses. Job stress can disrupt mood and sleep, and cause family and friendship relations to decline. People who experience chronic distress may have an increased risk of cardiovascular disease, musculoskeletal disorders, psychological disorders, workplace injuries, or other health related problems. Stressful working conditions are also associated with increased absenteeism, tardiness, and a desire to resign.[42]

Employers can reduce stress and adversity in the workplace. And by doing so, they can increase productivity and improve worker satisfaction. The National Institute for Occupational Safety and Health provides some suggestions for how managers may do that. For example, giving recognition for good work and high performance. Or, giving employees opportunities for career development and creating a workplace culture that values workers and their expertise. Or, clearly defining worker roles and responsibilities, and assigning an appropriate amount of work. And lastly, improving communication, providing opportunities for social interactions, and allowing workers to participate in decision-making.[42]

These solutions also require management to create and enforce policies, and educate management and workers on how to recognize, and safely address, these problems. Creating a workplace where workers are held accountable for their decisions, including giving credit for achievements and contributions, and investigating reports, can create a fair workplace. Anytime management receives a report, rather than simply believing or disbelieving the report, they should consider it evidence of a possible underlying problem. Management may, then, be able to create an acceptable resolution for the person filing the report by moving the person to a different team, or changing a company policy. In the meantime, they can they investigate the nature of the problem by collecting more evidence and information during a period of time.

When employers fail to take these measures, it creates a lot of unnecessary financial waste, harms the careers of workers, and puts the business in jeopardy, depending on the nature of the problem. They also risk losing some of their higher performing, and more talented, people. Not only are these measures better for employees, it helps the business to grow faster, be more successful, and can create a more loyal following among workers and customers.

5

Social Isolation Adversity

Social isolation, and loneliness, can be harmful, if not crippling, in some circumstances. But it does not have to. Having some time alone for thinking, reflecting, and personal development, can be beneficial to your mental health. Many great scientists, like seventeenth century Physicist and Mathematician Isaac Newton, or the twentieth century inventor Nikola Tesla, lived and worked in almost complete isolation, devoting their time and energy to their scientific studies, well into their eighties. When you have time on your hands, and you spend that time productively, you can accomplish many wonderful things. But social isolation, or loneliness, can also present significant challenges that can do harm and damage, and can become a form of adversity.

Instances of social isolation and loneliness are not uncommon and are believed to effect nearly one-fifth to half of the population. According to the U.S. Census, more than a quarter of the U.S. population lives alone, with fewer Americans getting married and having children. One report estimated that 79 percent of Generation Z and 71 percent of millennials felt lonely in comparison to 50 percent of boomers.[25]

According to studies of social isolation, extended periods of isolation or loneliness can cause a person's health to decline. Social isolation increases the risk of early death, similar to other health risks, like obesity, physical inactivity, or air pollution. Poor social connections increase the risk of diseases, like heart disease by 29 percent, and the risk of stroke by 32 percent. People who are socially isolated were found to have more instances of depression, poorer cognitive function, substance-related deaths, and suicide.[25]

Social support and personal relationships, in contrast,

were found to reduce distress, improve mental and physical health, and lower a person's mortality risk.[55] While these studies are certainly informative, it's even more essential to know the underlying reasons that explain the health disparities between socially isolated people and those who are not. For example, relationships tend to provide positive emotional reinforcement and positive memories to reflect on. Being in a relationship can improve communication skills, cooperation, storytelling, and facilitate the formation of new relationships. Being in a close relationship can create a greater sense of obligation to family, friends, or employers, which can give life greater meaning and purpose. Sometimes people are motivated to do things out of a sense of obligation, like keeping their homes clean when they expect company, or having a positive attitude toward those they live with.

Social isolation and loneliness, can cause a number of practical problems. Extreme social isolation can reduce trusting relationships and positive experiences, potentially creating more distressing experiences and memories. It creates a situation of not having someone to turn to in times of need, or not having the financial support to endure periods of unemployment. People who are socially isolated do not always cope with the isolation and loneliness in healthy ways. A socially isolated person may spend more time reflecting, and ruminating, on negative experiences, which creates more distress and negative attitudes. Social isolation can also drive negative self-talk, substance use, or overeating, which has compounding negative effects on a person's condition.

Reducing social isolation is not always easy. You will find people who are biased in believing that those who are socially isolated must have some undesirable defect, maybe the person is a liar. And that distrust can be even more socially isolating, and can lead to conflicts and more adversity.

You can mitigate the risks of social isolation by staying healthy and getting regular physical activity to prevent or reduce health related problems. Staying engaged in healthy activities may prevent negative self-talk or unhealthy coping mechanisms. Self-development and the pursuit of life goals can increase self-confidence, take your mind off negative experiences, and enable you to achieve goals that could improve your social status. And seeking to develop new and healthy relationships, either online or in-person, may reduce the perception of social isolation or loneliness.

6

Mental Disorders

One of the theories presented in this book is that the severe chronic distress created by severe forms of adversity, can cause certain types of mental disorders. You should also note that many mental disorders and syndromes also have biological origins, like brain infections, brain tumors, and brain injuries, which are known to cause Psychosis, Schizophrenia, hallucinations, and variety of other symptoms. When those conditions are correctly diagnosed by a trained and qualified professional, and treated within an adequate amount of time, the patient can have a quick return to health.

A *mental disorder* is an abnormal mental condition that disrupts, impairs, or interferes with the normal function of cognitive abilities, including your judgment and your ability to make good decisions. The U.S. Department of Health and Human Services has defined mental health as the ability to "cope with the stresses of life" and "be productive."

The inability to do either one of these things would severely cripple a person's ability to support oneself.

The costs and burdens of mental disorders on communities can be enormous. A study by the United States Department of Health and Human Services found that "mental and behavioral disorders and serious emotional disturbances (SEDs) in children and adolescents can lead to school failure, alcohol or illicit drug use, violence, or suicide." Untreated mental disorders, according to the study, cost in terms of "lost productivity due to illness, premature death, criminal justice interaction process, and property loss." During 1996, for example, almost $70 billion was spent in the United States treating and diagnosing mental disorders. Nearly $75 billion more was spent on disability insurance and lost productivity because of illness or deaths that were attributed to mental disorders. And another $6 billion was spent on property loss, law enforcement, and criminal justice because of mental disorders that same year.[12] During one year alone, depression cost the United States $40 billion due to lost productivity and health care costs, making it a "leading cause of absenteeism and diminished productivity" in the workforce.[12]

Mental disorders exist on a spectrum from mild to severe. And simply because a person has a mild mental disorder does not mean that person has a mental health problem. A person with a mild mental disorder, like a phobia or anxiety disorder, can live a very healthy and productive life. Anxiety disorders, like mood disorders, panic disorders, obsessive compulsive disorders, or social anxiety disorders, are statistically some of the most common.[12] Phobias that include a fear of heights, dark places, spiders, snakes, or social isolation, are mild mental disorders that are typically not harmful to a person's mental health, and may even have protective qualities.

Severe mental disorders, on the other hand, can significantly impair judgment and alter a person's state of mind. Severe mental disorders can overwhelm a person with emotions, and cause distorted perceptions and false beliefs, which can interfere with that person's ability to operate and interact with people. When a condition prevents the person from earning a living or forming relationships, that person's overall condition can decline overtime.

Severe depression, for example, can cause a person to have less confidence in one's abilities, greater self-doubt, greater despair, and may be more likely to give-up and throw away life opportunities. And that can cause a person to think about suicide more frequently. A mental disorder that is severe enough to threaten a person (e.g., suicidal tendencies), or other people (e.g., homicidal tendencies), is usually considered to be a mental health problem that requires treatment before it leads to hospitalization, incarceration, or death.

One theory about how adverse experiences, like being repeatedly victimized by an abuser, may cause a mental disorder, comes from the world of Behaviorism. Behaviorists studied how behavior develops as a result of conditioning, which is a process of developing behavior in response to repeated reinforcement. In the early decades of the 20th century, John Watson and Rosalie Rayner demonstrated this by attempting to condition an eleven-month-old child to fear animals. The child, who they called Albert, was introduced to a rat, rabbit, and a monkey, which were the neutral stimuli in the experiment. At first, Albert was unafraid, curious, and wanted to touch the animals. When the researchers surprised Albert by striking a steel bat with a hammer (i.e., the unconditioned stimulus) he began to cry. When the re-searchers combined the two in repeated experiments, and struck the bat in the presence of a rat, Albert's fear of the sound transferred to the rat. Basically, Albert learned to fear the rat. When researchers presented the rat without the sound, Albert would cry and crawl away. Albert's fear also transferred to other animals and developed into a general-ized phobia of other small animals, an effect they called stimulus generalization. Consequently, any animal caused Albert to cry and crawl away.[24] Watson and Raynor later suggested that this type of conditioning could influence a person's behavior long after the events occurred.[59]

This research suggests that repeated exposure to intense adverse experiences that evoke emotions, like fear, anger, conflict, or other intense emotional reactions, over an ex-tended period of time, strengthens those responses and changes the way a person responds to life circumstances. When those intense emotional reactions become habituated, it becomes more difficult to regulate and control those emo-tions. And if a deep emotional response is triggered by ad-verse experiences, and the person slips into an intense state of distress, it can interfere with productivity, relationships, and lead to poor life-altering decisions. Of course, that de-pends on how that person decides to cope with the disorder.

Adversity does not have to be intensely emotional to in-fluence a person's development. It can also exist in the form of discouragement, in which a child may be repeatedly told that he is not good enough, or "smart" enough. And that can chip-away at that child's self-confidence, one's ability to overcome life difficulties, which could lead to despairing and giving-up.

People who are at high risk of depression often face sig-nificant life difficulties. According to studies on depression, risk factors for depression include having a medical condition, like cancer or stroke, or a significant life change, like unemployment, financial problems, problematic relationships, or significant losses.[43] In all of these difficult situations, if the person is constantly distressed and pessimistic and wants to despair and give-up, that would be characteristic of depression.

Another common disorder that causes problems is substance use disorder, which has a variety of causes. A common characteristic of addiction is that the addict becomes preoccupied with anticipating the activity. But those activities also have a lot of negative side effects and negative consequences. Toxins impair judgment and decision-making, which results in faulty reasoning, reduced comprehension, poor coordination, avoiding personal interaction, difficulty concentrating, memory problems, and can cause a person to make terrible life-altering decisions.

The more time a person spends intoxicated, the more difficulty that person will have performing roles, responding to events, solving problems, cooperating with people, achieving goals, and may have a greater number of health, legal, and financial problems. Side-effects of substance use can happen suddenly, like being arrested for committing a crime while intoxicated. Or they can accumulate during many years. Frequent substance use can have cumulative side-effects, like social avoidance, the inability to perform work related responsibilities, and a decline in self-confidence, which makes a person vulnerable to verbal criticism, mental insecurity, and feeling like one is under constant attack, which creates even more adversity. The more frequently a person engages in risky behaviors, the more likely one is to experience the negative social, financial, or legal consequences associated with the activity.

When severe forms of adversity, like child abuse, are caught early, the abuse can be recognized and the victim can begin to recover. But when it's not recognized, it can do damage to the victim physically and mentally that can result in mental and behavioral problems. When others see that damage, they usually don't recognize it and assume it must be a defect, or a fault of their own. And they may be quick to automatically put responsibility on that person for any problems one is experiencing, which creates more adversity.

Therapy is a common recommended treatment if you are experiencing distress or a decline in your mental or physical health. That is especially true if you are experiencing mental disorders, or problems that create significant distress. It can help treat problems with emotional instability, declining productivity, strained relationships, sleep deprivation, trauma, and addictions.

7
Critical Skills

Adversity can be one of the most destructive forces on a person's mental health. And understanding how specific actions, beliefs, or biases, create adversity in people's lives, and how that adversity creates distress and mental health problems, can help you in your judgment of other people and in your interpretation of their behavior. If have problems controlling your anger and you are a parent, you may want to see a therapist because you don't want to create unnecessary adversity that could be harmful to your child's development and future. If you are a manager, you need to spot behaviors that negatively affect the stability and operation of the organization and work to police those problems.

Actively reducing unnecessary adversity and excessive stress, can reduce many social problems, like a decline of mental health, domestic abuse, diminished life satisfaction, and others.

The ability to tolerate personal differences can enable you to work more effectively with people in driving your success. All people have a different appearance, different values, different styles, different life pursuits, different way of life, and different opinions that you may disagree with. Most of these differences are beyond your ability to control. So, trying to force people to conform to your thinking, and your way of life, or by excluding or punishing them for not doing so, can create unnecessary stress and adversity. It tends to ruin productive relationships, decrease cooperation and wealth, and makes everyone poorer and less satisfied as a result.

When judging another person (e.g., for an employment opportunity), instead of focusing on small details gleaned from a small amount of information, try to look at the bigger picture at what the person has accomplished and the type of work that person is capable of performing. Too often, hiring managers focus on small, insignificant, details. Instead, you should try to look beyond singular things the person says, or uncertain details from the person employment history, and focus more on the person's accomplishments and what it takes to accomplish those things. That will give you a better idea about the person's work ethic and will give that person fairer consideration in the job market.

If you are an organizational manager, try to actively reduce stress in the workplace by setting rules, policies, and expectations for acceptable behavior, and enforce those rules. Have reasonable expectations for the type, and amount, of work assigned to workers to avoid creating too much stress. Make sure workers are being treated with respect. And if workers are not being treated fairly, look into what it takes to resolve those problems. Make sure they are okay mentally and physically, and that they are satisfied in their job roles, to create and maintain a healthy and productive organization.

If you are experiencing excessive distress or mental health problems, Therapy can help work through those problems. If you are facing your problems alone, your attention may be drawn more to the adversity you are experiencing, rather than focusing on more productive activities. By having someone to talk to, who may be able to provide expert advice and help guide you in a positive direction.

My hope is that combining all of the different critical thinking skills introduced in this book, from assessing your own judgment, to your responsibility, capabilities, motives, and your mental health, should give you a good start in making positive change, not only in your life, but in the lives of other people.

REFERENCES

1. Adler, A. (1949). Understanding Human Nature. (W. B. Wolfe, M.D., Trans.). (pp. 8, 134). New York: Permabooks. (Original work published 1927)
2. American Humane. (n.d.). Emotional Abuse. Retrieved April 8, 2007, from http://www.americanhumane.org
3. American Institute of Stress. (n.d.). Job Stress. Retrieved March 31, 2007, from http://www.stress.org/job.htm
4. American Institute of Stress. (n.d.). Stress, Definition of Stress, Stressor, What is Stress?, Eustress?. Retrieved March 31, 2007, from http://www.stress.org/americas.htm
5. Angwin, J., Larson, J., Mattu, S., Kirchner, L., Machine Bias. ProPublica. Retrieved January 27, 2018 from https://www.propublica.org/article/machine-bias-risk-assessments-in-criminal-sentencing
6. Cannon, W. B. (1963). Bodily Changes in Pain, Hunger, Fear and Rage. (2nd ed., pp. 195, 243-244). New York: Harper Torchbooks. (Original work published 1920)
7. Carnahan, B. Moore, C. (July 07, 2020). Actively Addressing Unconscious Bias In Recruiting. Harvard Business School. Retrieved May 11, 2021 from

https://www.hbs.edu/recruiting/blog/post/actively-addressing-unconscious-bias-in-recruiting

8. Christina Bethell, PhD, MBA, MPH; Jennifer Jones, MSW; Narangerel Gombojav, MD, PhD; Jeff Linkenbach, EdD; Robert Sege,MD, PhD. (September 9, 2019). Positive Childhood Experiences and Adult Mental and Relational Health in a Statewide Sample. Associations Across Adverse Childhood Experiences Levels. JAMA Pediatrics. (Volume 173, Number 11). Retrieved January 3, 2020 from https://jamanetwork.com/journals/jamapediatrics/fullarticle/2749336

9. Corbin, C. B., Corbin, W. R., Welk, G. J., & Welk, K.A. (2006). Concepts of Fitness and Wellness: A Comprehensive Lifestyle Approach (6th ed., p. 295). University of Central Oklahoma. Boston: McGraw-Hill Custom Publishing

10. Dalio, R. (September 19, 2017). Principles: Life and Work. Simon & Schuster.

11. Department of Health and Human Services. (2000, November). Healthy People 2010: Understanding and Improving Health (2nd ed), p. 26-3. Washington, DC: U.S. Government Printing Office.

12. Department of Health and Human Services. (2000, November). Healthy People 2010: Understanding and Improving Health (2nd ed), pp. 18-3 – 18-5, 18-15, 18-19, 18-20, 18-26. Washington, DC: U.S. Government Printing Office

13. Duhigg, C. (February 25, 2016). What Google Learned From Its Quest to Build the Perfect Team. The New York Times. Retrieved April 17, 2016

from http://www.nytimes.com/2016/02/28/maga-
zine/what-google-learned-from-its-quest-to-build-
the-perfect-team.html

14. Duhigg, C. (February 28, 2012). The Power of
    Habit: Why We Do What We Do in Life and Busi-
    ness. Random House.

15. Dweck, C. (February 28, 2006). Mindset: The New
    Psychology of Success. Random House; 1 edition.

16. Ericsson, A. (April 11, 20017). Peak: Secrets from
    the New Science of Expertise. Eamon Dolan Books
    Paper.

17. Ferris State University. (n.d.). Anti-Black Imagery.
    Jim Crow Museum of Racist Memorabilia. Re-
    trieved May 13, from https://www.fer-
    ris.edu/HTMLS/news/jimcrow/antiblack

18. Freud, S. (1950). Totem and Taboo. (J. Strachey,
    Trans.). (Standard ed., p. 63). New York: Norton.
    (Original work published 1913)

19. Fromm, E. (1990). The Sane Society. (p. 65). New
    York: Owl Books. (Original work published 1955)

20. Harris Interactive. (May 31 - June 17, 2001). Atti-
    tudes in the American Workplace VII. The Seventh
    Annual Labor Day Survey. Telephone Polling for
    The Marlin Company by Harris Interactive. Re-
    trieved May 16, 2021 from
    https://www.stress.org/wp-content/up-
    loads/2011/08/2001Attitude-in-the-Workplace-Har-
    ris.pdf

21. Heathfield, S. (October 11, 2017). The 2 Most Im-
    portant Management Secrets: Pygmalion and Gala-
    tea Effects. The Balance. Retrieved December 17,
    2017 from https://www.thebalance.com/pygmalion-
    and-galatea-effects-1918677

22. Heerema, E. (January 05, 2020). How Poor Judgment Can Be a Sign of Early Dementia. Verywellhealth. Retrieved May 11, 2021 from https://www.verywellhealth.com/poor-judgment-and-alzheimers-disease-98564

23. Hock, Roger R. (2002). Forty Studies that Changed Psychology: Explorations into the History of Psychological Research. 4th ed. Upper Saddle River, New Jersey: Prentice Hall

24. Hock, Roger R. (2002). Forty Studies that Changed Psychology: Explorations into the History of Psychological Research. 4th ed. (pp. 71-72). Upper Saddle River, New Jersey: Prentice Hall

25. Holt-Lunstad, J. (June 22, 2020). Social Isolation And Health. Health Affairs Health Policy Brief, June 22, 2020. DOI: 10.1377/hpb20200622.253235. Retrieved May 16, 2021 from https://www.healthaffairs.org/do/10.1377/hpb20200622.253235/full/brief-social-isolation-mortality-Holt-Lunstad.pdf

26. Innocence Project. (n.d.). False Confessions or Admissions. Retrieved September 2, 2016 from http://www.innocenceproject.org/causes/false-confessions-admissions

27. Investopedia. (n.d.). Gambler's Fallacy. Retrieved March 19, 2016 from http://www.investopedia.com/terms/g/gamblersfallacy.asp

28. Keshner, A. (August 4, 2020). Most white people don't believe racial discrimination exists at their workplace, but nearly half of black employees disagree. MarketWatch. Retrieved May 13, 2021 from https://www.marketwatch.com/story/the-people-who-handle-racial-discrimination-complaints-in-

the-workplace-are-divided-on-how-big-of-a-prob-lem-it-is-2020-08-03

29. Konnikova, M. (November 18, 2013). On the Face of It: The Psychology of Electability. The New Yorker. Retrieved April 17, 2016, from http://www.newyorker.com/tech/elements/on-the-face-of-it-the-psychology-of-electability

30. Landau, E. (February 10, 2009). Study: Experiences make us happier than possessions. CNN. Retrieved April 23, 2016 from http://www.cnn.com/2009/HEALTH/02/10/happi-ness.possessions

31. Letter to Bishop Mandell Creighton (April 5, 1887). Transcript of, published in Historical Essays and Studies, edited by J. N. Figgis and R. V. Laurence (London: Macmillan, 1907)

32. Lewsley, J. (July 28, 2020). What are the effects of racism on health and mental health? MedicalNews-sToday. Retrieved May 13, 2021 from https://www.medicalnewstoday.com/articles/ef-fects-of-racism

33. Likierman, Sir A., (January-February 2020). The El-ements of Good Judgment: How to Improve Your Decision-Making. Harvard Business Review. Re-treived May 11, 2021 from https://hbr.org/2020/01/the-elements-of-good-judg-ment

34. Livingston, S. (January 2003). Pygmalion in Man-agement. Harvard Business Review. Retrieved on December 17, 2017 from https://hbr.org/2003/01/pygmalion-in-management

35. Loftus, E. F. (1975). Leading questions and the eye-witness report. Cognitive Psychology, 7(4), 560-572.

36. Machiavelli, N. (1966). The Prince. (D. Donno, Trans.). (p. 70). New York: Bantam Dell. (Original work published 1532)
37. Maden, J. (December 2020). Socrates and the Socratic Paradox: I Know That I Know Nothing. Retrieved June 2, 2021 from https://philosophybreak.com/articles/socrates-and-the-socratic-paradox-i-know-that-i-know-nothing
38. Maslow, A. H. (1976). The Farther Reaches of Human Nature. (pp. 26, 117). New York: Penguin.
39. Mayo Clinic. (2006, June 26). Tips for Coping with Stress. Retrieved March 30, 2007, from http://www.mayoclinic.com/health/coping-with-stress
40. McEwen, B., & Seeman, T. (1999, August). Allostatic Load and Allostasis. MacArthur Network on SES & Health. Retrieved December 14, 2006, from http://www.macses.ucsf.edu/Research/Allostatic/notebook/allostatic.html
41. Morse, G. (January 2006). Decisions and Desire. The Harvard Business Review. Retrieved August 4, 2018, from https://hbr.org/2006/01/decisions-and-desire
42. National Institute for Occupational Safety and Health. (n.d.). Stress ...At Work. U.S. Department of Health and Human Services, Public Health Service, Centers for Disease Control and Prevention, National Institute for Occupational Safety and Health. Retrieved May 16, from https://www.cdc.gov/niosh/docs/99-101/pdfs/99-101.pdf
43. National Institute of Mental Health (NIMH). (2006, September 13). Depression. Retrieved March 31,

2007, from http://www.nimh.nih.gov/publicat/de-pression.cfm

44. Pew Research Center. (October 30, 2014). People in Emerging Markets Catch Up to Advanced Econo-mies in Life Satisfaction: Asians Most Optimistic about Future, Middle Easterners the Least. Re-trieved April 3, 2016 from http://www.pewglobal.org/2014/10/30/people-in-emerging-markets-catch-up-to-advanced-econo-mies-in-life-satisfaction

45. Pink, D. (April 5, 2011). Drive: The Surprising Truth About What Motivates Us. Riverhead Books

46. Pinsker, J. (October 23, 2014). Does Inequality Cause Crime? New research suggests that what matters isn't disparity itself, but whether people are flaunting their riches. The Atlantic. Retrieved May 24, 2021 from https://www.theatlantic.com/busi-ness/archive/2014/10/does-inequality-cause-crime/381748

47. PRNewswire. (February 27, 2020). IBM Survey: Only 38% of State and Local Government Employ-ees Trained on Ransomware Prevention. Retrieved May 20, 2021 from https://news-room.ibm.com/2020-02-27-IBM-Survey-Only-38-of-State-and-Local-Government-Employees-Trained-on-Ransomware-Prevention

48. Reed, W. & Schanzenbach, M. (1996). Chapter 27: OSHA - We're From the Government and We're Here to Help You. Prices and Information: A Sim-ple Framework for Understanding Economics. Re-trieved April 1, 2007, from http://www.ou.edu/class/econ3003/book/area1c27.html

49. Robson, N. (November 23, 2014). Oklahoma Watch: Number of homeless children in Oklahoma is among highest in nation. NewOK.com. Retrieved July 6, 2017 from http://newsok.com/article/5369190

50. Rock, D., Grant, H. (November 04, 2016). Why Diverse Teams Are Smarter. Harvard Business Review. Retrieved May 11, 2021 from https://hbr.org/2016/11/why-diverse-teams-are-smarter

51. ScienceDirect. (n.d.). Expectancy-Value Theory. Retrieved June 3, 2021 from https://www.sciencedirect.com/topics/psychology/expectancy-value-theory

52. Thaler, R., Sunstein, C. (February 24, 2009). Nudge: Improving Decisions About Health, Wealth, and Happiness. Penguin Books.

53. The Muse. (March 19, 2013). The Secret to Motivating Your Team. Forbes. Retrieve April 16, 2016 from http://www.forbes.com/sites/dailymuse/2013/03/19/the-secret-to-motivating-your-team/#597d4255433f

54. Turner, C. (MARCH 11, 2015). The Teenage Brain: Spock Vs. Captain Kirk. Retrieved March 12, 2015, from http://www.npr.org/blogs/ed/2015/03/11/391864852/the-teenage-brain-spock-vs-captain-kirk

55. Umberson, D., Montez, J. K. (2010) Social Relationships and Health: A Flashpoint for Health Policy. Journal of Health and Social Behavior. Retrieved September 7, 2015 from http://hsb.sagepub.com/content/51/1_suppl/S54.full.pdf

56. United States Holocaust Memorial Museum, Washington, DC. (nd). Nazi Propaganda. United States Holocaust Memorial Museum. Retrieved May 13, 2021 from https://encyclopedia.ushmm.org/content/en/article/nazi-propaganda

57. Vincent J. Felitti, MD, FACP, Robert F. Anda, MD, MS, Dale Nordenberg, MD, David F. Williamson, MS, PhD, Alison M. Spitz, MS, MPH, Valerie Edwards, BA, Mary P. Koss, PhD, James S. Marks, MD, MPH) (1998) Relationship of Childhood Abuse and Household Dysfunction to Many of the Leading Causes of Death in Adults. The Adverse Childhood Experiences (ACE) Study. American Journal of Preventive Medicine. p. 1. Retrieved January 2, 2020 from https://www.ajpmonline.org/article/S0749-3797(98)00017-8/pdf

58. Visser, S. (June 12, 2016). Euro 2016: Dozens injured as crowds of rival fans brawl. CNN. Retrieved June 12, 2016 from http://www.cnn.com/2016/06/11/world/euro-2016-england-russia-brawl

59. Watson, J. B., & Rayner, R. (1920). Conditioned emotional responses. Journal of Experimental Psychology, 3

INDEX

abilities,
consequential, pp. 109-110
measuring, pp. 107-108
ability,
capacity of, p. 108
measurement of, p. 135-137
abuse, fight-or-flight response, p. 229
accepting loss, p. 214
accountability,
criminal justice, p. 92
defined, p. 92
systems of, pp. 92-94
Adler, Alfred, excuses, p. 76
Adverse Childhood Experiences, pp. 224-225
adversity spectrum, pp. 221-222
adversity, p. 8
behavioral problems, p. 223
crime, p. 163
defined, p. 200
discouragement, p. 223
effects of, p. 222-223
employment, pp. 234-237
social isolation, pp. 238-240
Affordable Care Act, p. 96
Alzheimer's disease, p. 22
analysis,
cost-benefit, pp. 54-57
scenario, pp. 52-53
anger, character defense, p. 74
answering for decisions, pp. 72-73
anxiety disorders, p. 241
artificial intelligence, pp. 57-60
attitude, pp. 216-217
attributing responsibility, p. 68
attribution error, defined, p. 66
At-Will employment laws, pp. 97-98
authority, obedience to, p. 90
bad judgment, cause of, p. 5
Bandura, Albert, social learning theory, p. 183
Becker, Gary, crime, pp. 162-

163
behavioral adaptation, p. 109
behavioral change, p. 118
    habits, p. 124
    incentives, pp. 180-181
    skills, p. 124
Berkley, George, perception, p. 40
blaming, pp. 75-77
bounded rationality, p. 38
brain health, pp. 22-23
brand reputation, pp. 178
Cannon, Walter, anger, p. 74
capacity of ability, p. 108
Casey, B. J., p. 21
changing expectations, p. 177
character defenses, pp. 73-74
    defined, p. 74
character development, p. 129-130
character, defined, p. 129
child maltreatment, pp. 225-226
childhood adversity, pp. 224-230
childhood, responsibility, p. 224
choice, defined, p. 37
choices, pp. 37-39
chronic stress, pp. 210-212
cognitive focus,
    immediate interests, p. 169
    productivity, pp. 168-169
cognitive limitations, pp. 16-35
commitment, motivation, pp. 184-185
communication skills, pp. 191-192
competitive rivalry, p. 234
computer programming, pp. 29-30
confidence assessment, pp.

132-134
conflict resolution skills, pp. 196-198
controlling attention, p. 177
cooperation, motivation, pp. 189-198
corporate social responsibility, p. 87
corruption,
    defined, p. 88
    incompetence, p. 90
    power, p. 89
cost-benefit analysis, pp. 54-57
creativity, pp. 174-176
criminal justice, accountability, p. 92
critical decisions, defined, pp. 11-12
critical thinking skills, p. 11
Dalberg-Acton, John, corruption, p. 89
Dalio, Ray, data models, p. 58
Damasio, Antonio, p. 21
data modeling, pp. 57-60
data models, errors, p. 31
deception, pp. 78-80
    defined, p. 78
decisions, answering for, pp. 72-73
default options, p. 39
delegating responsibility, pp. 83-84
developmental solutions, pp. 114-116
DHEA, p. 206
discouragement,
    life circumstances, p. 113
    motivation, pp. 181-184
distress,
    behavioral problems, p. 206
    fear, pp. 207-209

Duhigg, Charles, habits, pp. 121-122

Dweck, Carol,
    encouragement, p. 183
    mindsets, pp. 111-114

Ebbinghaus, Hermann, learning curve, p. 131

Eccles, Jacquelynne, motivation, p. 149

economic injustice, defined, p. 163

economic value, p. 152

egalitarian values, p. 222

emotional skills, pp. 192-194

emotional stressors, p. 206

emotions, pp. 25-26
    motivation, pp. 158-161

employment adversity, pp. 234-237

encouragement,
    motivation, pp. 181-184
    parenting, p. 128

enlightenment, path to, p. 36

Ericsson, K. Anders, expertise, p. 120

error checking, pp. 49-50

eustress, p. 205

executive ability, pp. 20-23

Expectancy-Value Theory, p. 149

expectations, motivation, p. 150

external locus, p. 70

extrinsic rewards, p. 179

fear, distress, pp. 207-209

fight-or-flight response, p. 208
    abuse, p. 229

fixed mindset, p. 111

Freud, Sigmund, delusion of persecution, pp. 76-77

Fromm, Eric, rationalization, pp. 77-78

Functional Magnetic Resonance Imaging, p. 137

gains,
    motivation, pp. 155-158
    productivity, pp. 155-158

Galatea effect, p. 194

Gambler's Fallacy, p. 32

Gestalt psychology, p. 174

get-trough-on-crime laws, p. 95

Gilovich, Thomas, happiness, pp. 160-161

giving responsibility, pp. 83-84

goal setting,
goal-setting, p. 148
    motivation, pp. 170-171

gossip, pp. 42-45

gradual improvement, principle of, p. 119

growth mindset, p. 111

habit, defined, p. 121

habits, pp. 121-122

habituation, p. 123

happiness, wealth, pp. 159-160

harmful biases, pp. 230-234

healthy relationships, pp. 190-191

heroism, p. 106

Hierarchy of Needs, p. 146

homo sapiens, p. 1

Howell, Ryan, happiness, pp. 160-161

human capital, pp. 125, 154

human condition, defined, p. 105

human resources, bad judgment, pp. 3-4

human studies, problem of, p. 107

I-35 bridge collapse, p. 96

immediate interests, cognitive focus, p. 169

impaired judgment, stress, p. 205

improving judgment, pp. 45-48

incentive based, motivation, pp. 178-181

incentive system, p. 93

incentives,
    behavioral change, pp. 180-181
      motivation, pp. 146-147
      problem of, p. 180

incompetence, corruption, p. 90

inequity, pp. 161-165

information, quality of, pp. 39-40

ingroup bias, pp. 44, 231

interest, defined, p. 150

interests, motivation, p. 150

internal locus, pp. 71-72

intrinsic rewards, p. 178

intuition, pp. 26-29
    role of, p. 42

job satisfaction, productivity, pp. 184-185

judgment,
    behavior, p. 10
    role of, p. 1

justice, defined, p. 161

Kahneman, Daniel,
    biases, p. 28
    heuristics, pp. 27-28
    loss aversion, pp. 178, 157-158

knowledge-based judgment, p. 18

labor laws, p. 97

leadership, pp. 4-5

learning curve, pp. 131-132

learning responsibility, pp. 67-68

leveraging time, p. 173

life circumstances, discouragement, p. 113

Likierman, Andrew, good judgment, pp. 13-15

Limbic System, p. 21

listening, communication, p. 191

Livingston, J. Sterling, management, p. 182

Locke, Edwin,
    goal-setting, p. 170
    motivation, p. 148

Loftus, Elizabeth, memory, p. 23

logical errors, pp. 30-33

loss,
    accepting, p. 214
    frustration p. 214
    motivation, pp. 155-158
    productivity, pp. 155-158

Machiavelli, Niccolo, p. 79

management skills, p. 128

management, testing, pp. 140-141

mandatory sentencing laws, p. 95

market value, p. 152

marketing, pp. 177-178

Maslow, Abraham, motivation, p. 146

Maslow, Abraham, sufficient knowledge, p. 47

measuring abilities, pp. 107-108, 135-137

meditation, p. 218

memory, pp. 23-25

mental disorders, pp. 240-245
    costs of, p. 241
    severe, p. 242

mental health, pp. 221-246
    self-confidence, pp. 110-111

mental ledger, p. 92
mental logic, pp. 29-30
mental models, pp. 17-19
    limitations, pp. 19-20
merit system, p. 93
Merton, Robert, crime, p. 163
metacritical thinking skills, p. 11
metacritique, p. 11
modeling techniques, pp. 51-52
monetary exchange value, p. 153
moral judgment, p. 50
motivating others, pp. 176-178
motivation, pp. 145-165
    commitment, pp. 184-185
    cooperation, pp. 189-198
    discouragement, pp. 181-184
    encouragement, pp. 181-184
    expectations, p. 150
    gains, pp. 155-158
    goal setting, pp. 170-171
    incentive based, pp. 178-181
    incentives, pp. 146-147
    interests, p. 150
    losses, pp. 155-158
    productivity, pp. 167-185
    selfishness, p. 151
    selflessness, p. 151
    wants, p. 151
natural talent, p. 108
Newton, Isaac, social isolation, p. 238
obedience to authority, p. 90
objective reality, pp. 40-41
obstruction, pp. 80-81
    defined, p. 80
open source, value, p. 179
optimizing, p. 38
over-confidence, p. 134

parenting skills, p. 128
parenting, encouragement, p. 128
Penalty Avoidance Benefit, p. 156
persecution, delusion of, pp. 76-77
personal responsibility, pp. 65-84
Pink, Daniel, motivation, pp. 178-179
Plato, p. 16
policy decisions, problem of, p. 95
political social responsibility, p. 88
Positive Childhood Experiences, p. 225
positive thinking, pp. 215-216
power of expectations, p. 194
power,
    corruption, p. 89
    responsible use of, pp. 88-92
Prefrontal Cortex, p. 21
    impairment, p. 22
prejudgment, p. 49
prejudice, p. 49
principle of gradual improvement, p. 119
principles, defined, p. 130
Private Interest Theory, pp. 149-152
private interest, p. 149
productivity,
    economics, p. 168
    gains, pp. 155-158
    goal setting, pp. 170-171
    losses, pp. 155-158
    motivation, pp. 167-185
    time management, pp. 171-174

Project Aristotle, p. 195

Pygmalion effect, pp. 182, 194

quality of information, defined, p. 40

racial hatred, p. 232

Rational Choice Theory, p. 148

rationalization, pp. 77-78

Rayner, Rosalie, conditioning, p. 242

reality test, defined, p. 60

reality testing, pp. 60-61

recreation, pp. 217-219

relationships,
    benefits of, p. 189
    trust, pp. 194-196

repression, defined, p. 81

research methods, pp. 36-63

research, improving judgment, pp. 45-48

resilience, p. 215

responsibility,
    attributing, p. 68
    defined, p. 66
    delegating, pp. 83-84
    denying, p. 73
    forms of, p. 66
    giving, pp. 83-84
    learning, pp. 67-68
    personal, pp. 65-84
    scope of, p. 69
    social, pp. 86-100
    taking, pp. 81-83

responsible policy, pp. 94-98

results-driven approach, p. 60

rewards,
    extrinsic, p. 179
    intrinsic, p. 178

risk mitigation, pp. 54-57

role model, skills development, p. 127

role modelling, p. 183

role skills, pp. 127-129

Roosevelt, Delano, p. 207

Rosenthal, Robert, Pygmalion effect, p. 182

Ross, Dorothea, social learning theory, p. 183

Ross, Sheila, social learning theory, p. 183

rumors, problem of, p. 43

satisficing, p. 38

scapegoat, defined, p. 76

scenario analysis, pp. 52-53

science, information source, p. 46

Scientific Method, p. 42

scope of responsibility, p. 69

self-confidence,
    defined, pp. 132-133
    mental health, pp. 110-111

self-doubt, benefit of, p. 133

self-fulfilling prophecy, p. 194

selfishness, motivation, p. 151

selflessness, motivation, p. 151

self-medication, p. 228

serious emotional disturbances, p. 241

severe depression, p. 242

severe mental disorders, p. 242

shared interest, p. 149

Simon, Herbert, bounded rationality, p. 38

skills deficits, problem of, p. 126

skills development, pp. 118-141

skills tests, pp. 138-141

skills, pp. 125-127

social bias, chronic distress, p. 212

social injustice, defined, p. 163

social isolation, adversity, pp. 238-240

social power, defined, p. 88
social pressure, influence of, p. 44
social problems, p. 8
    defined, p. 2
social responsibility, pp. 86-100
    corporate, p. 87
    defined, p. 87
    political, p. 88
Socrates, p. 16
Socratic Paradox, p. 16
stress management techniques, pp. 212-213
stress management, pp. 204-218
stress, impaired judgment, p. 205
stress, workplace, p. 235
stressors, pp. 209-210
    emotional, p. 206
studies, improving judgment, pp. 45-48
subjective experience, pp. 40-41
sufficient knowledge, p. 47
sunk cost, p. 158
Sunstein, Cass, default options, p. 39
suspending judgment, pp. 48-49
systems of accountability, pp. 92-94
taking responsibility, pp. 81-83
teamwork, p. 195
technology, responsible use of, pp. 99-100
Tesla, Nikola, social isolation, p. 238
testing effect, p. 139
testing, management, pp. 140-141
testing, training, p. 141

Thaler, Richard, default options, p. 39
time management, productivity, pp. 171-174
Todorov, Alexander, biases, p. 231
training, testing, p. 141
trust, relationships, pp. 194-196
Tversky, Amos,
    biases, p. 28
    heuristics, pp. 27-28
    loss aversion, pp. 178, 157-158
under-confidence, p. 134
unfairness, defined, p. 161
value creation, pp. 152-155
value driver, p. 154
value,
    economic, p. 152
    market, p. 152
    monetary exchange, p. 153
value-based judgment, p. 18
values, defined, p. 18
wants, motivation, p. 151
Watson, John, conditioning, p. 242
wisdom, meaning of, p. 1
Wright, Theodore P., learning curve, p. 131

INDEX

www.ingramcontent.com/pod-product-compliance
Lightning Source LLC
Chambersburg PA
CBHW061005280326
41935CB00009B/844